*"That love is inexhaustible,
you will be there"*

*forever*

_____

_____

_____

_____

_____

_____

THIS BOOK

*Belongs to*

_____

_____

# Visit Our Author Page At
## amazon.com

**Scan me**

# CRUISE SHIP COLORING BOOK

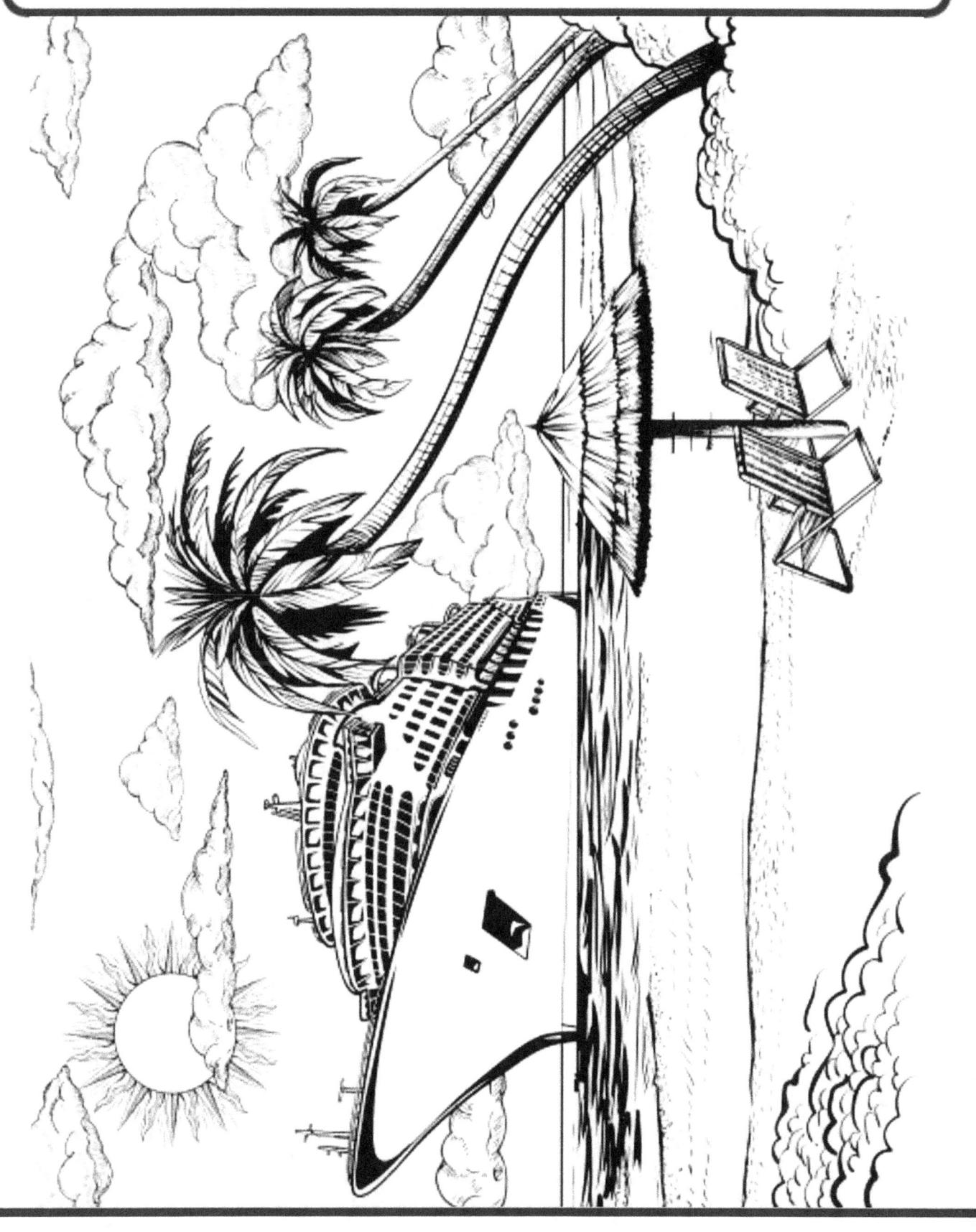

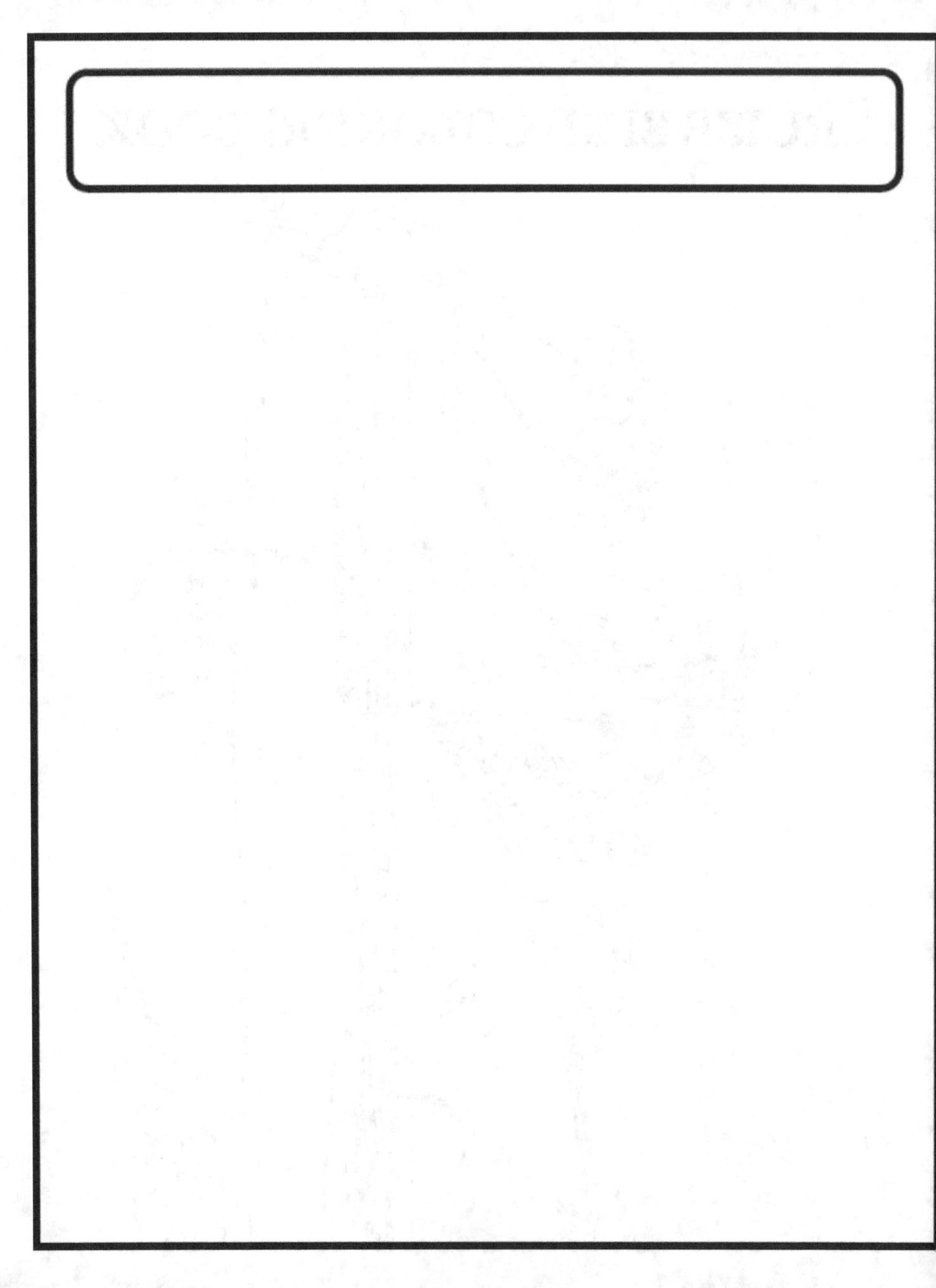

# CRUISE SHIP COLORING BOOK

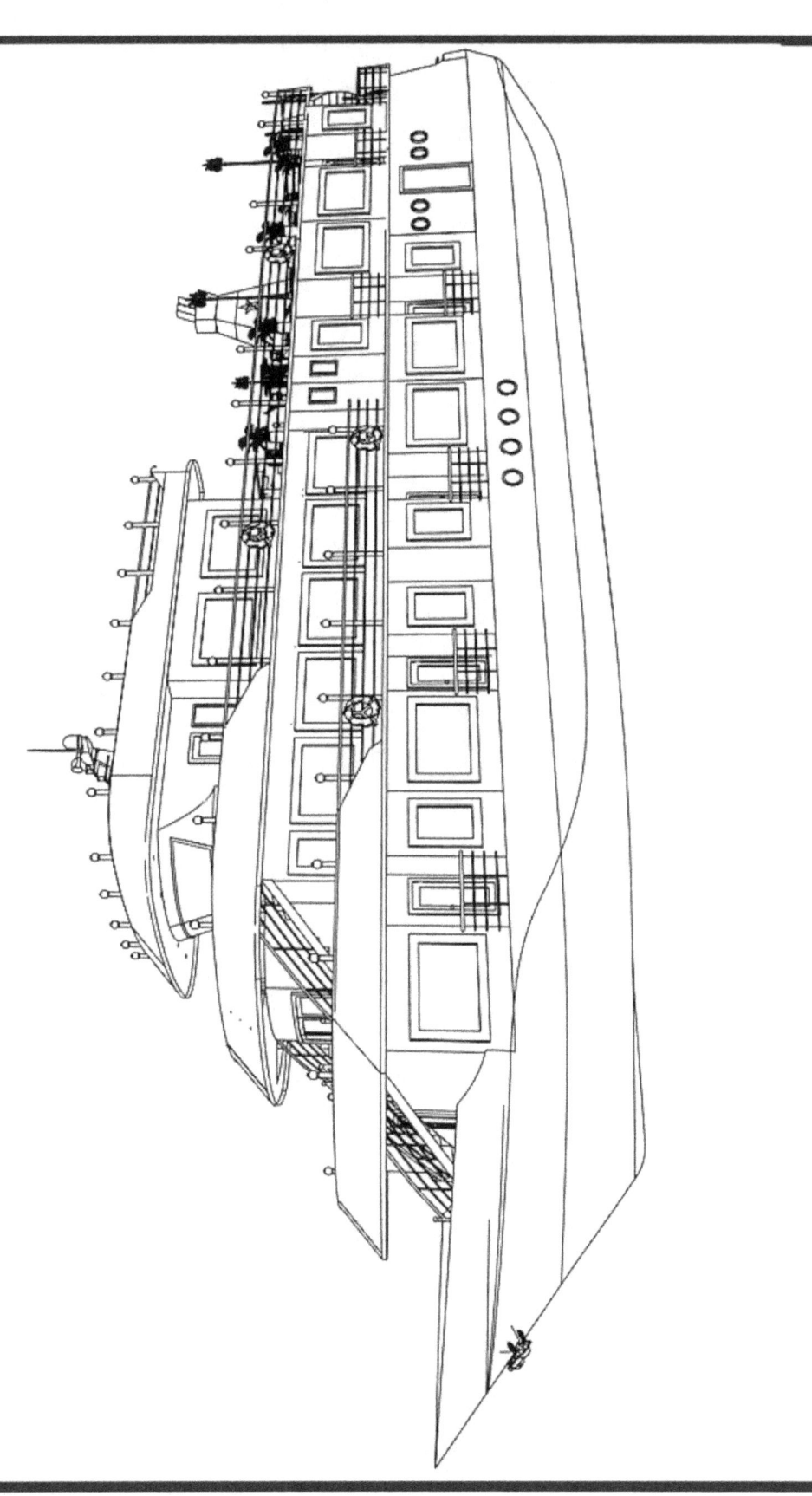

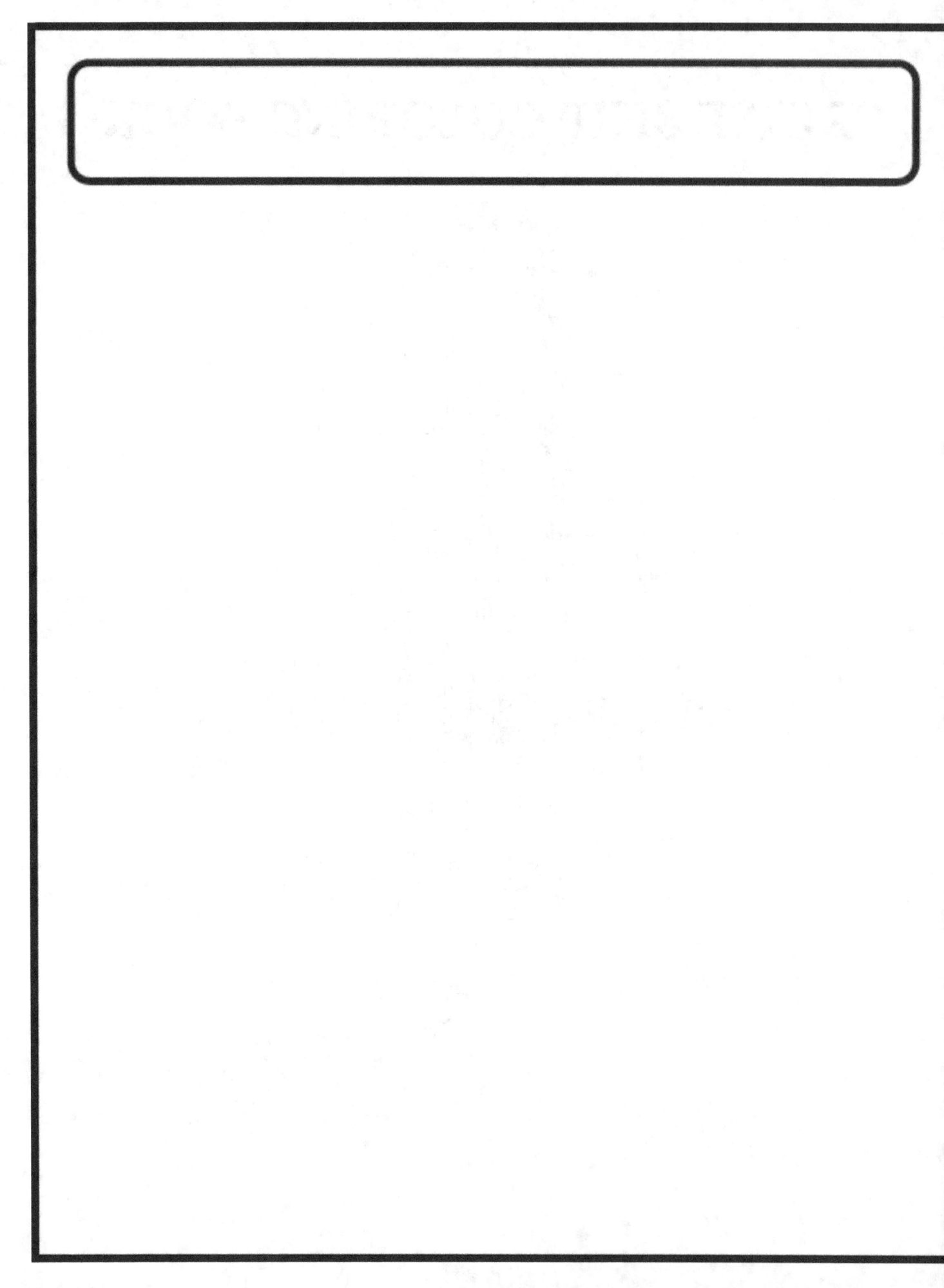

# CRUISE SHIP COLORING BOOK

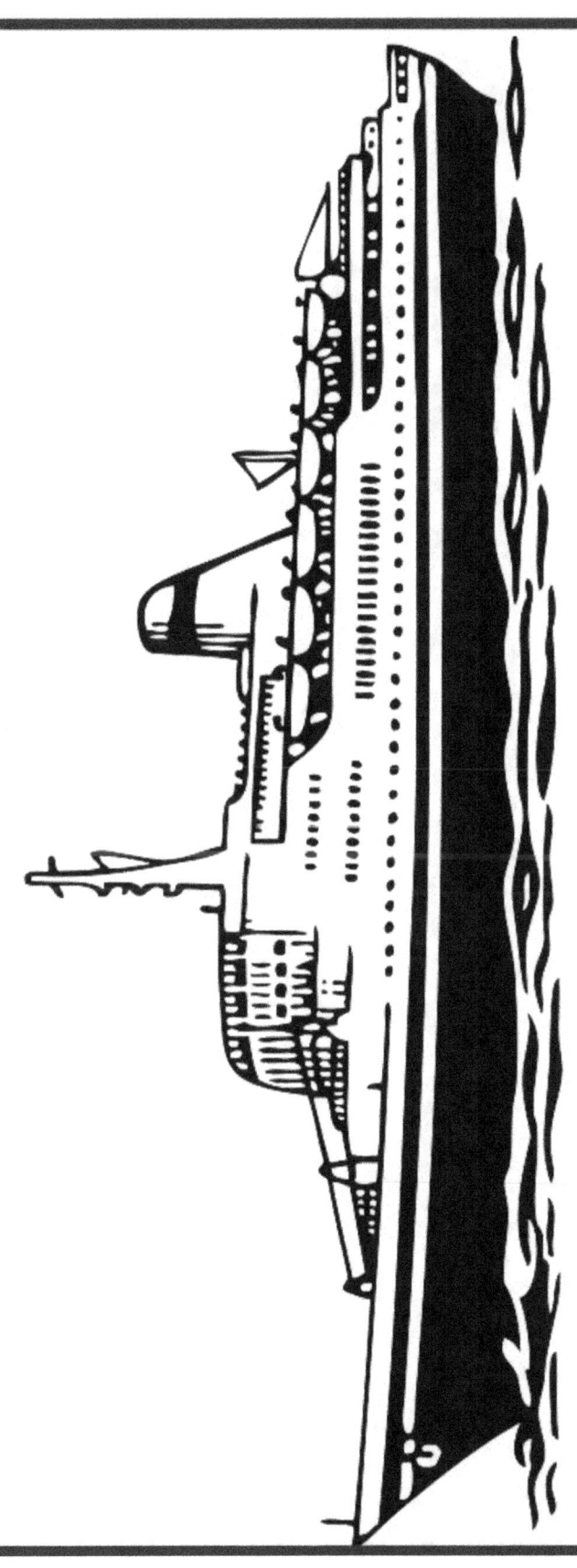

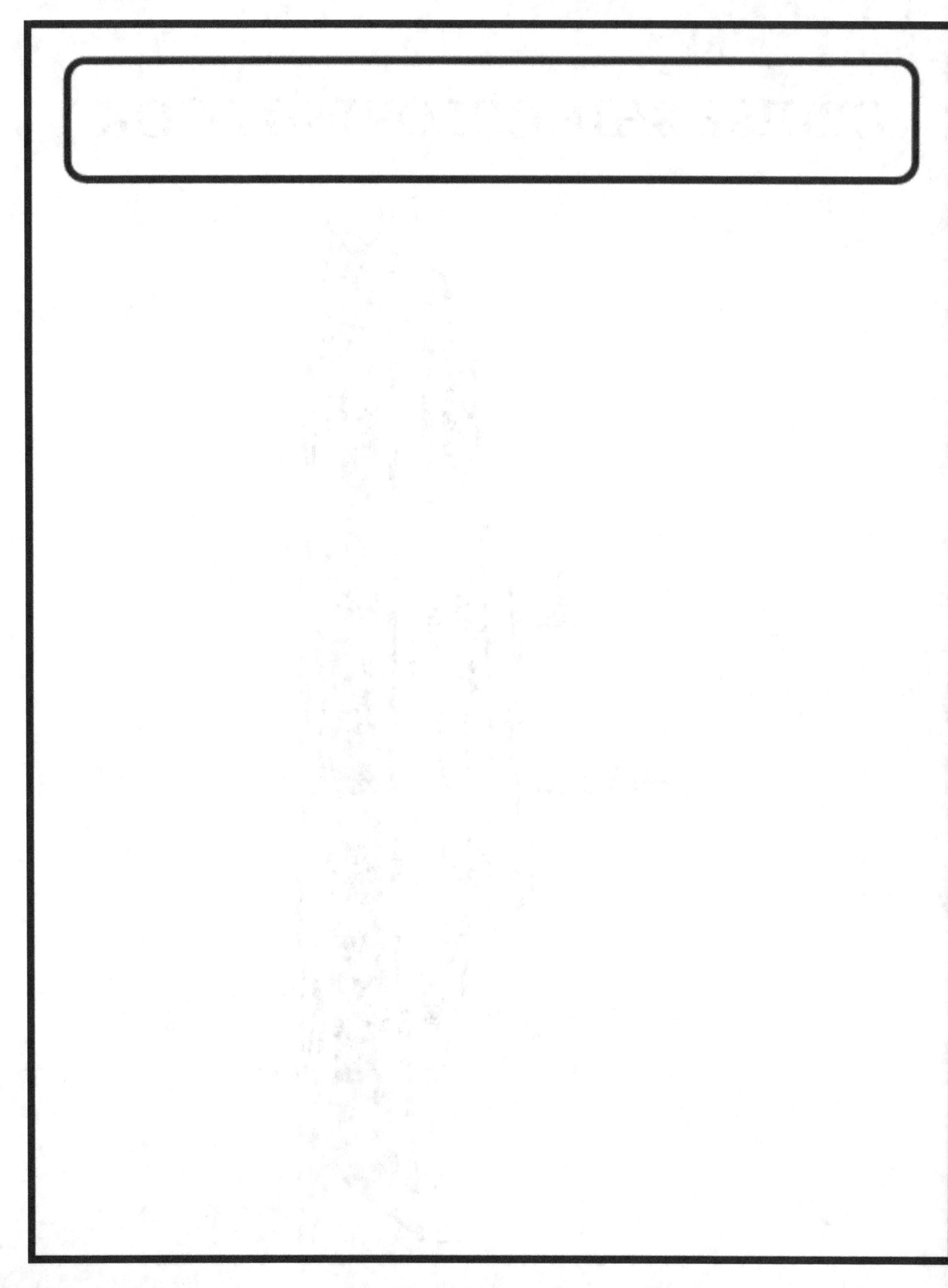

# CRUISE SHIP COLORING BOOK

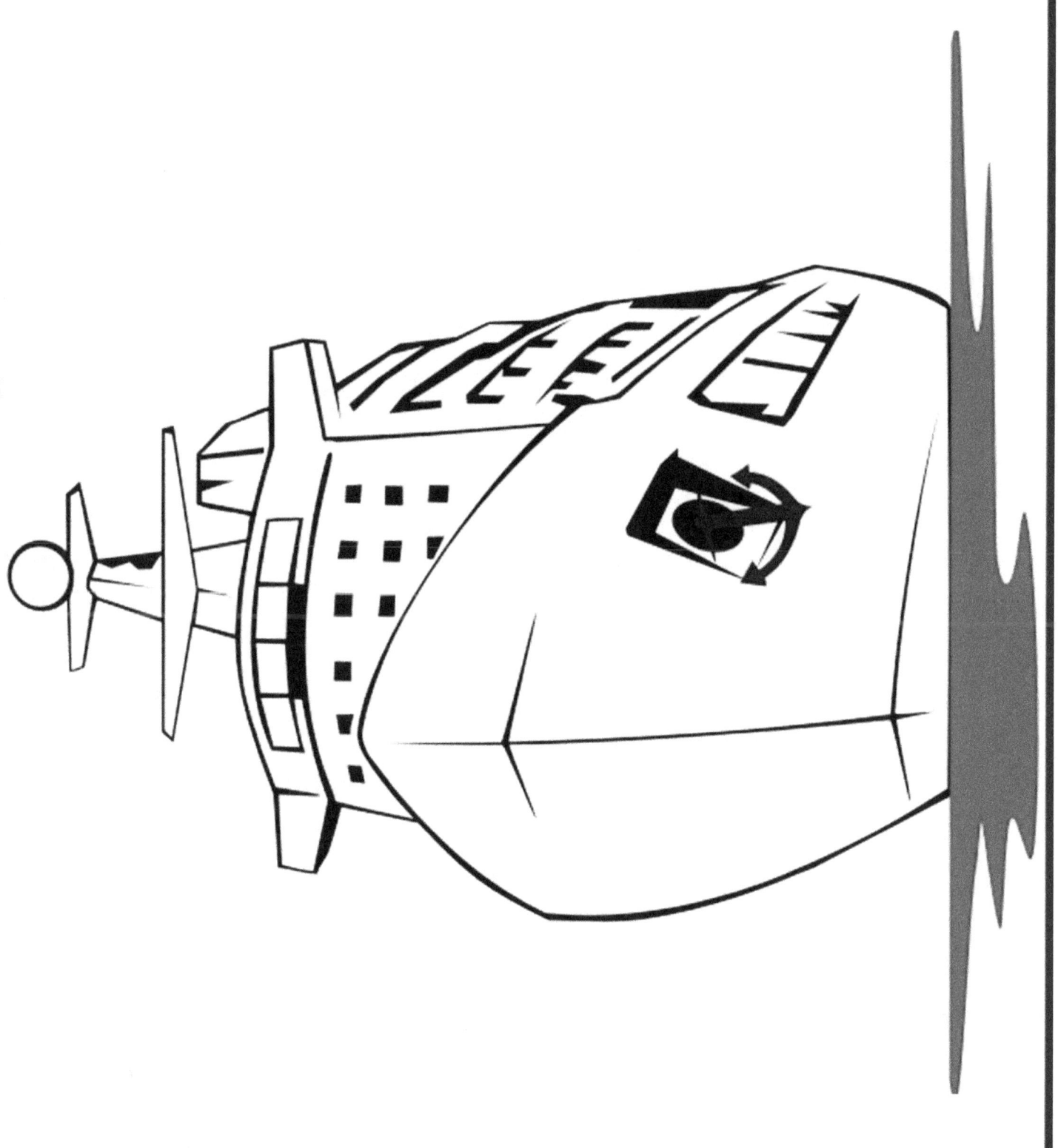

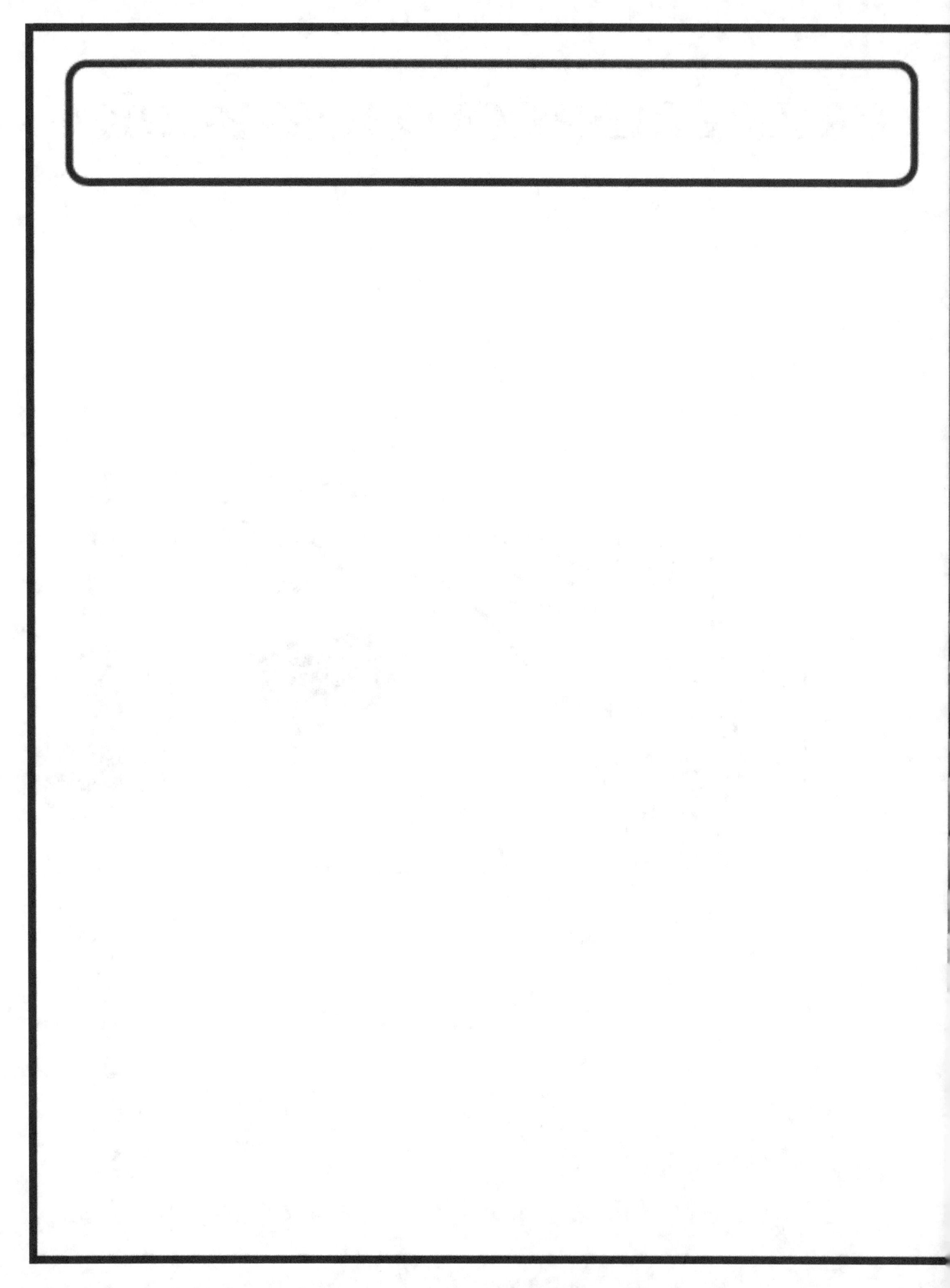

# CRUISE SHIP COLORING BOOK

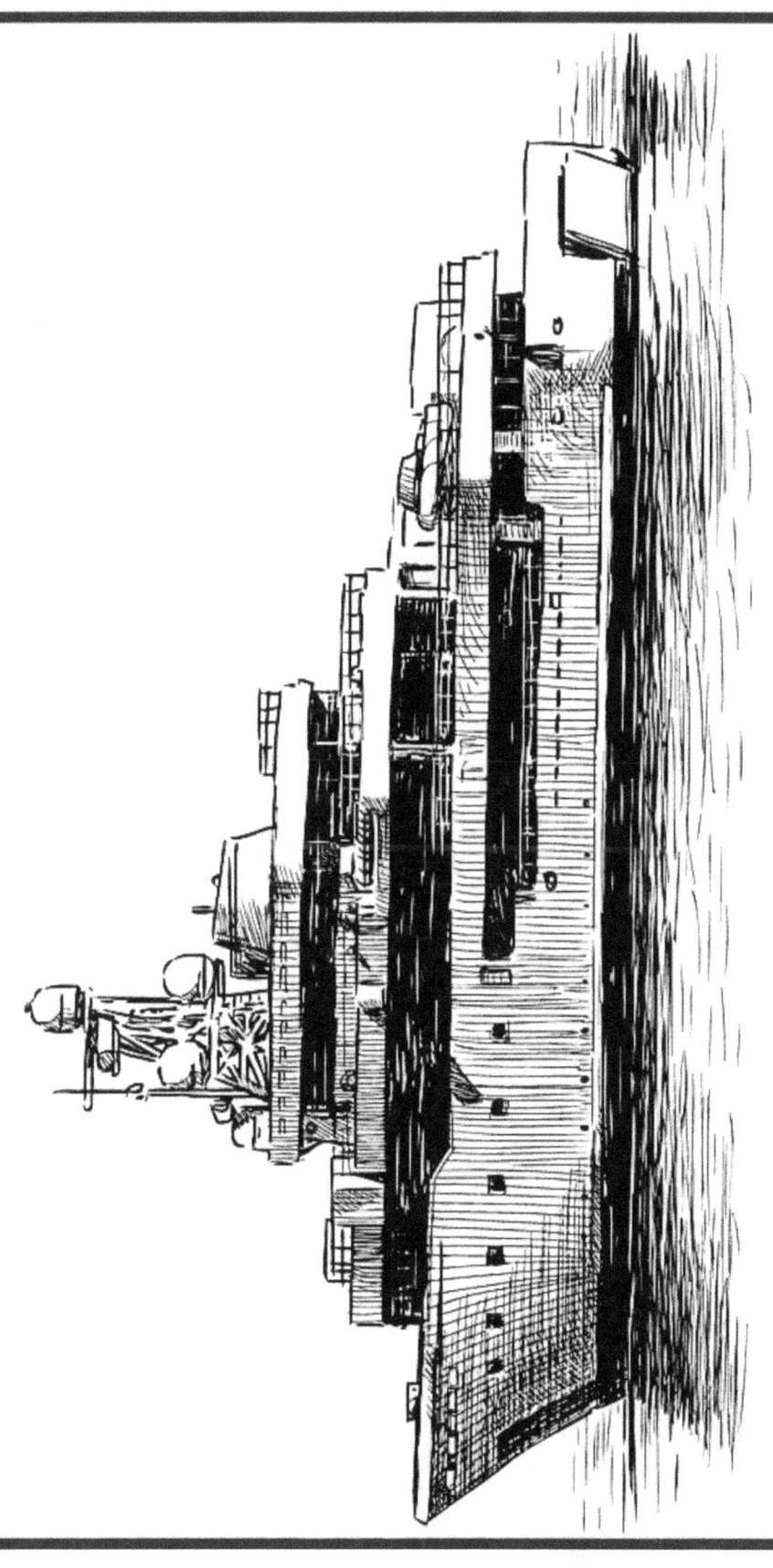

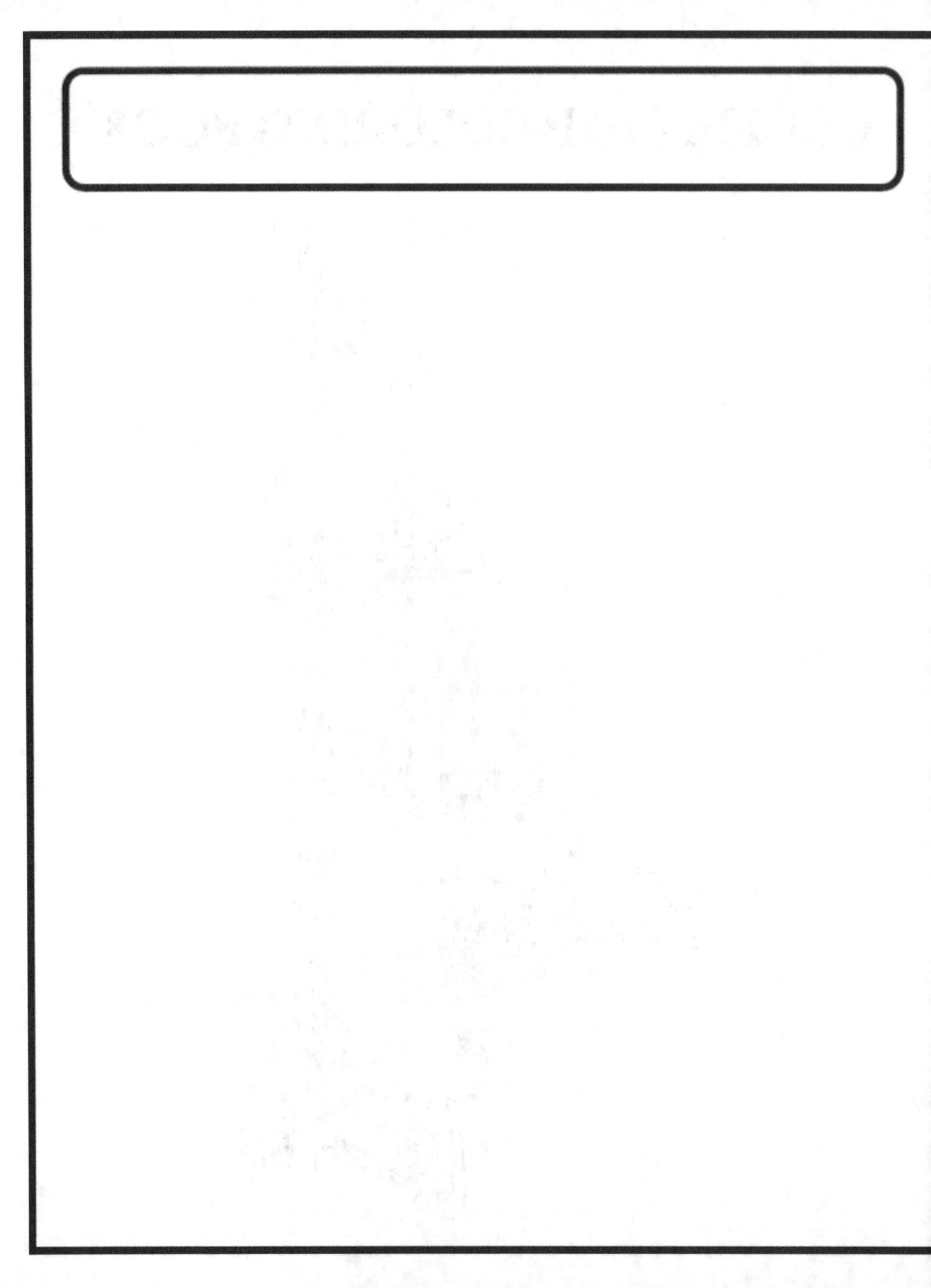

# CRUISE SHIP COLORING BOOK

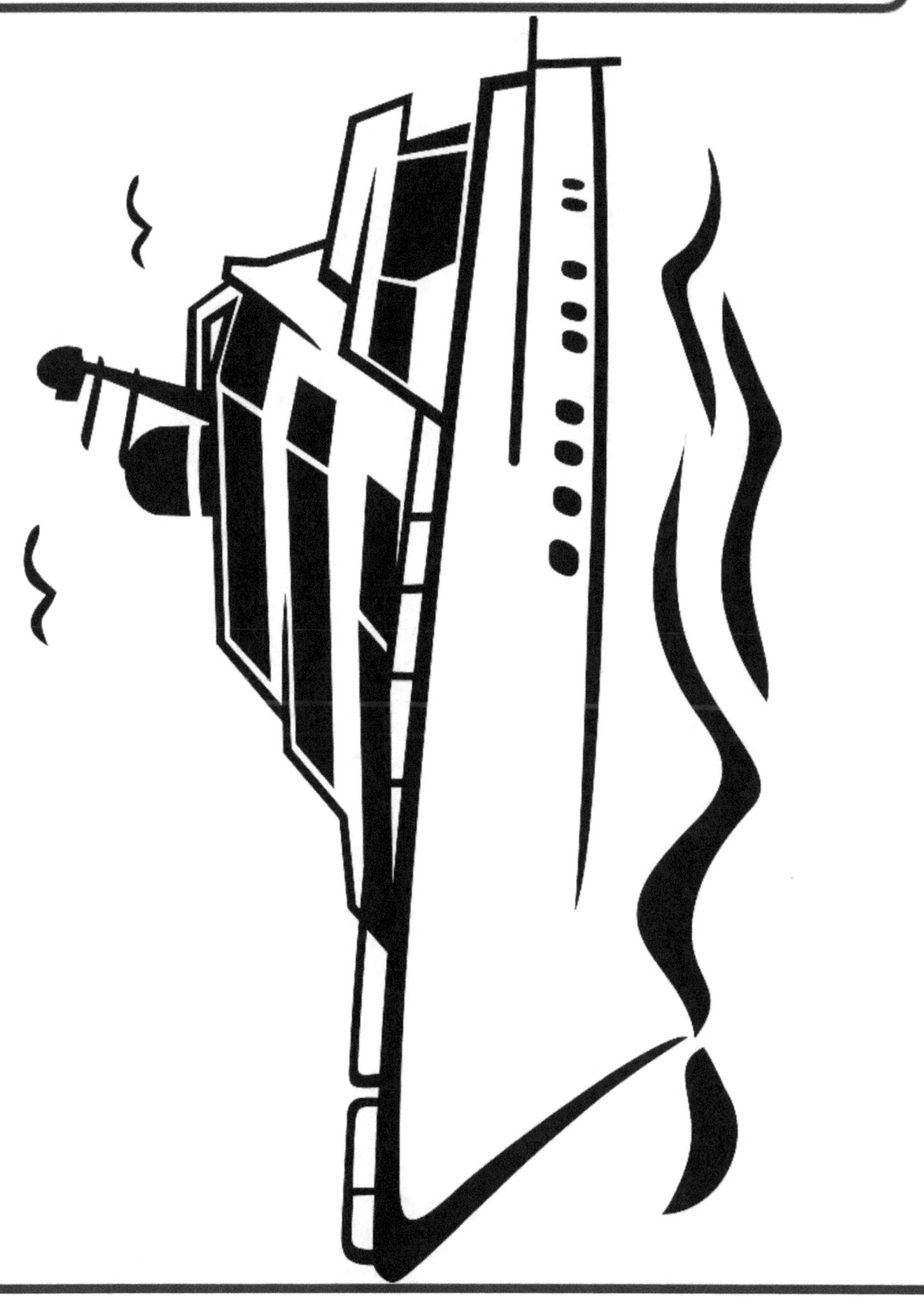

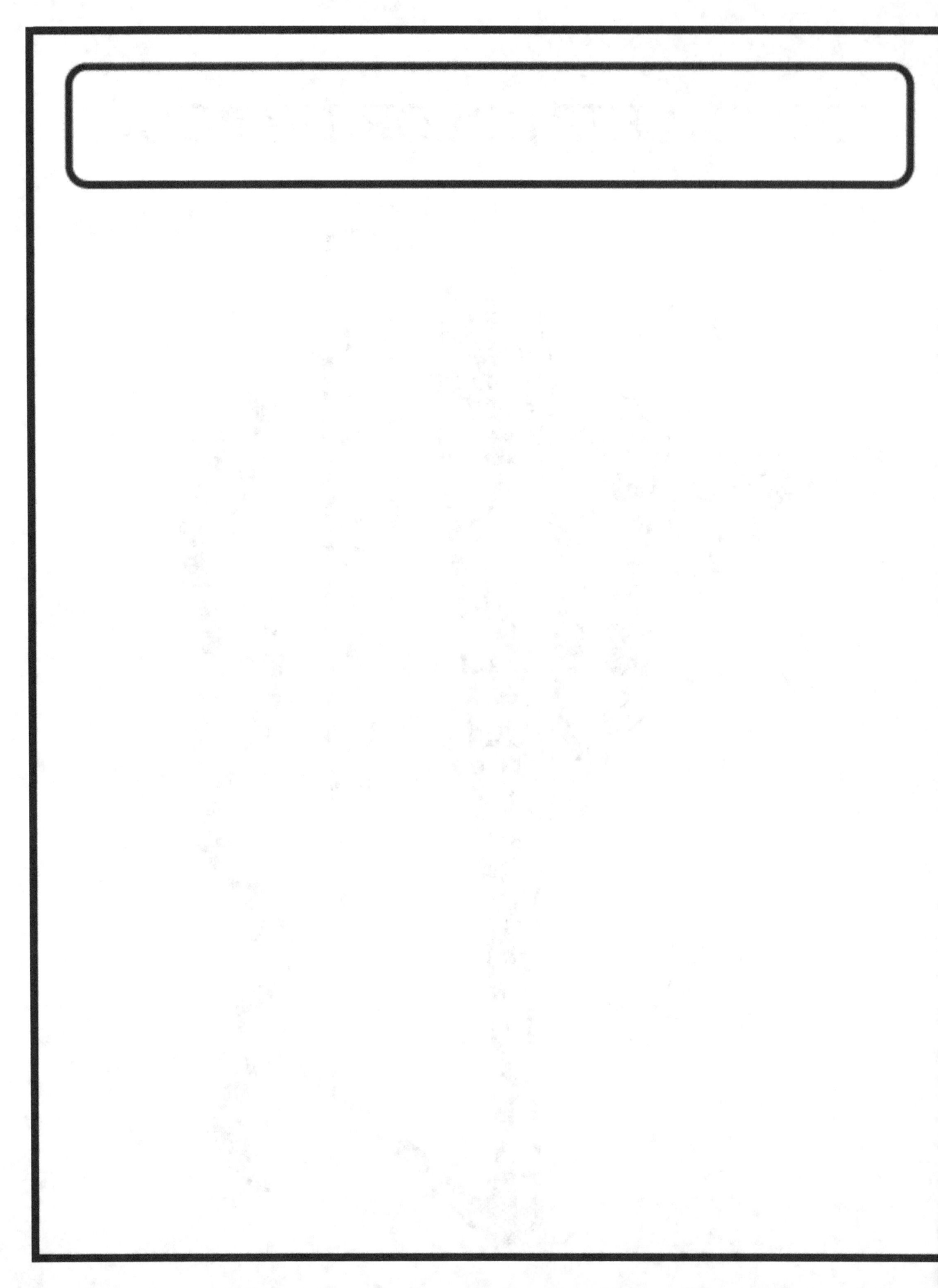

# CRUISE SHIP COLORING BOOK

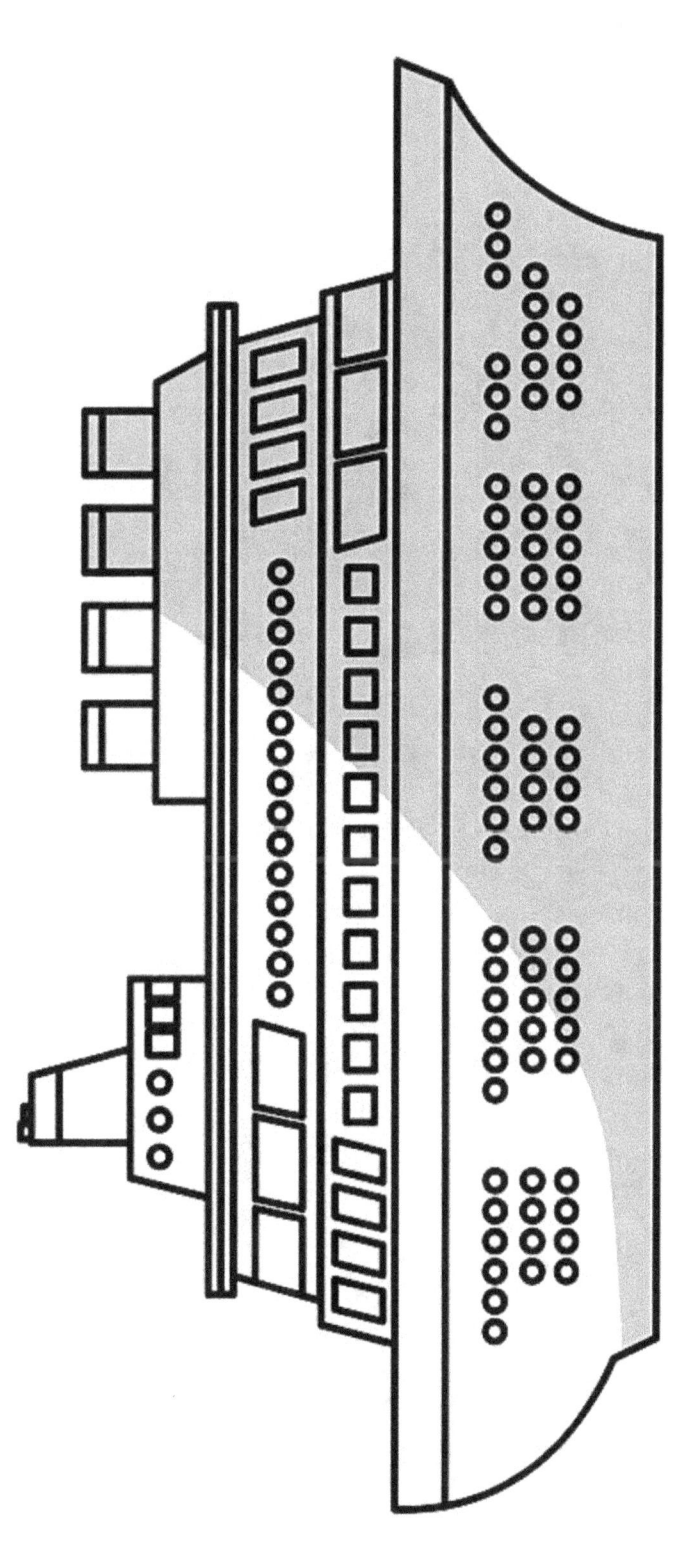

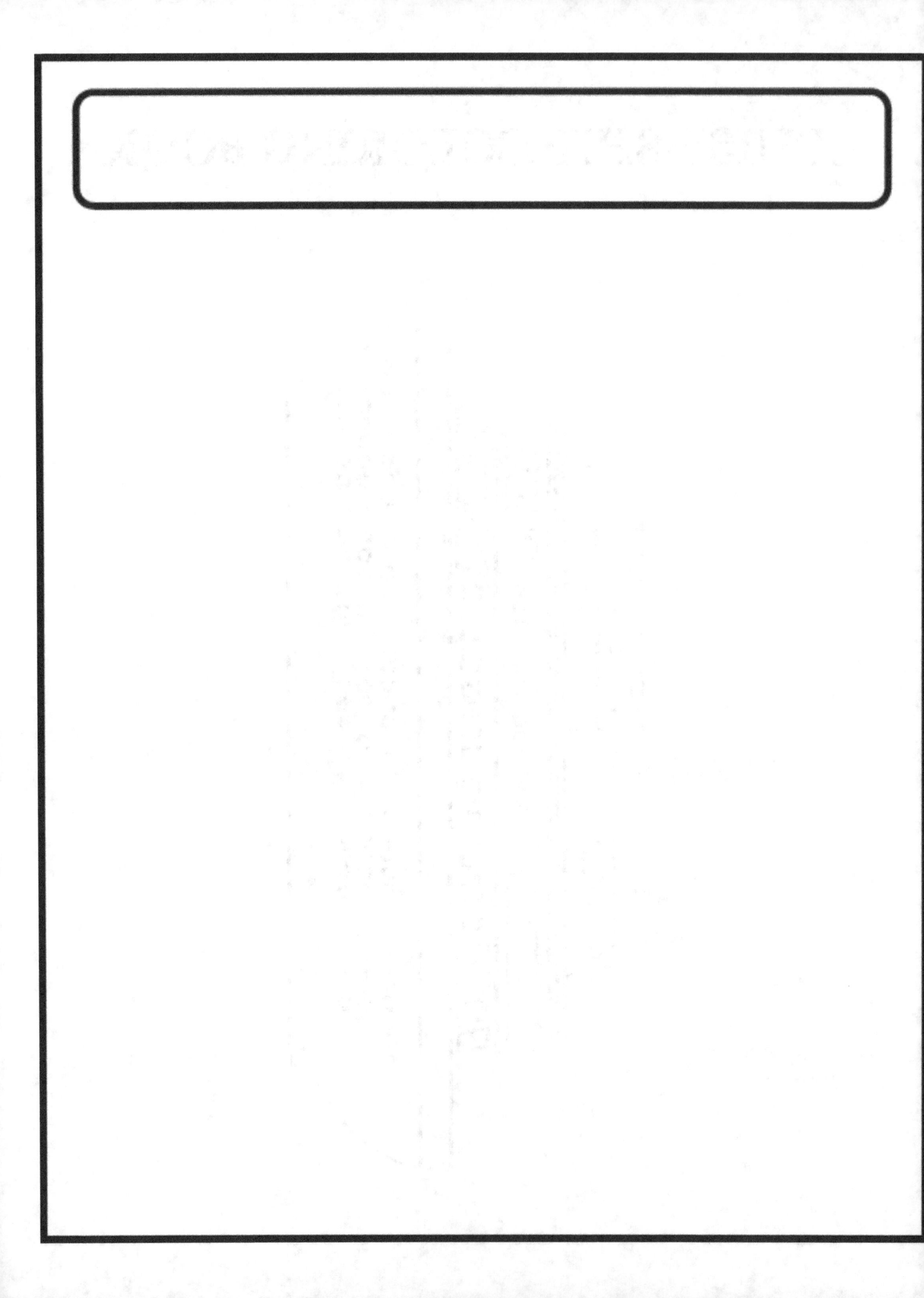

# CRUISE SHIP COLORING BOOK

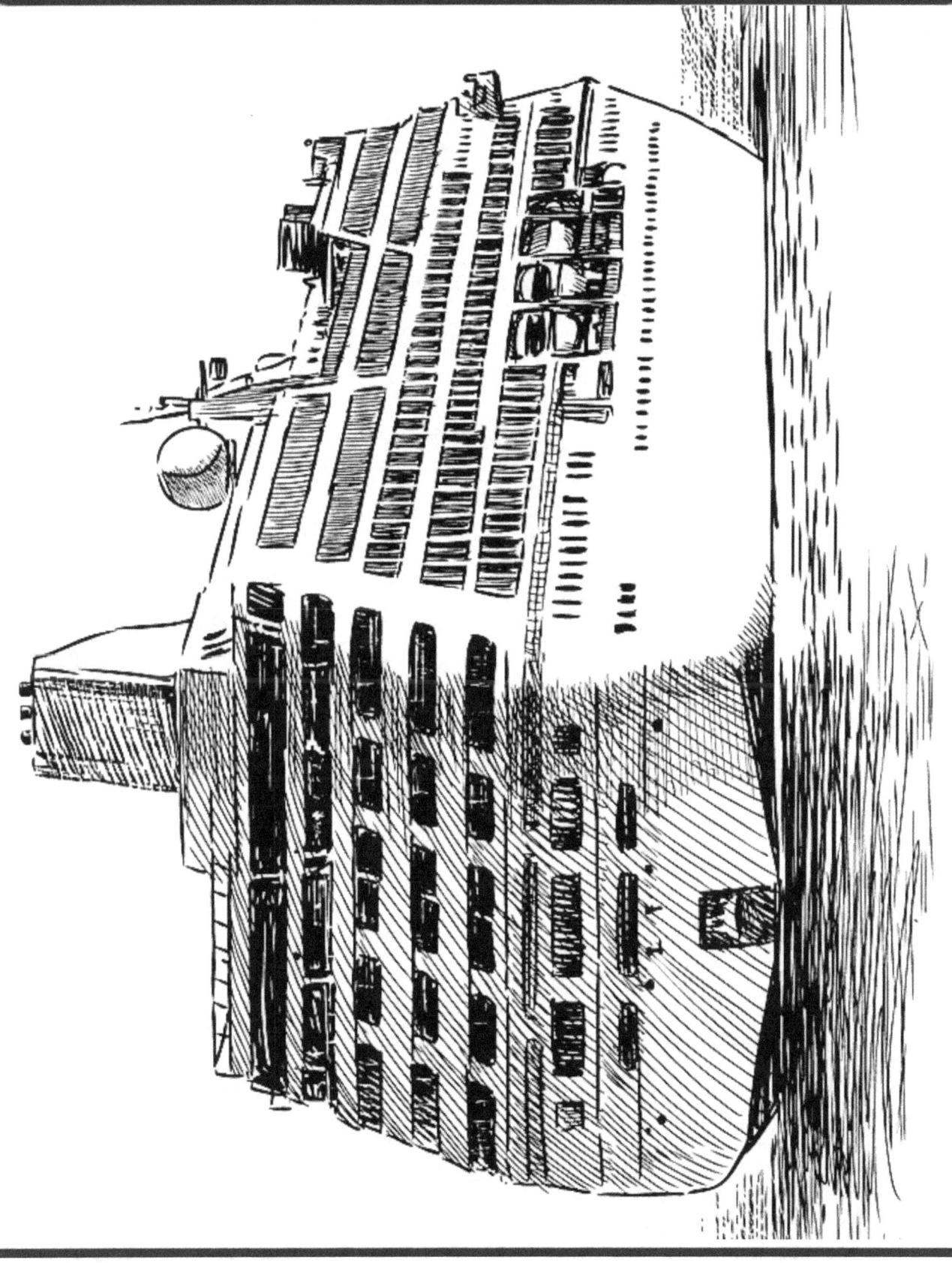

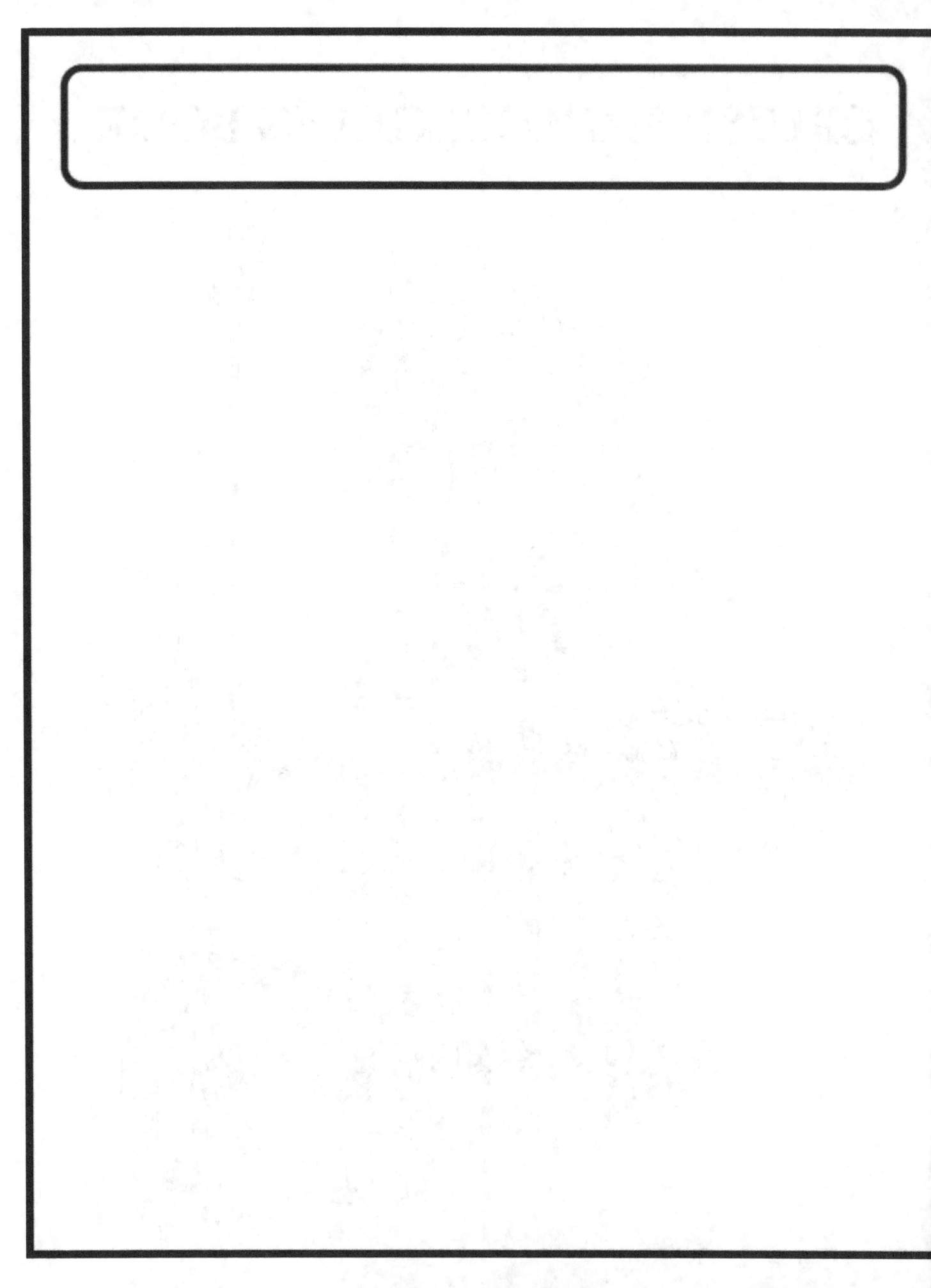

# CRUISE SHIP COLORING BOOK

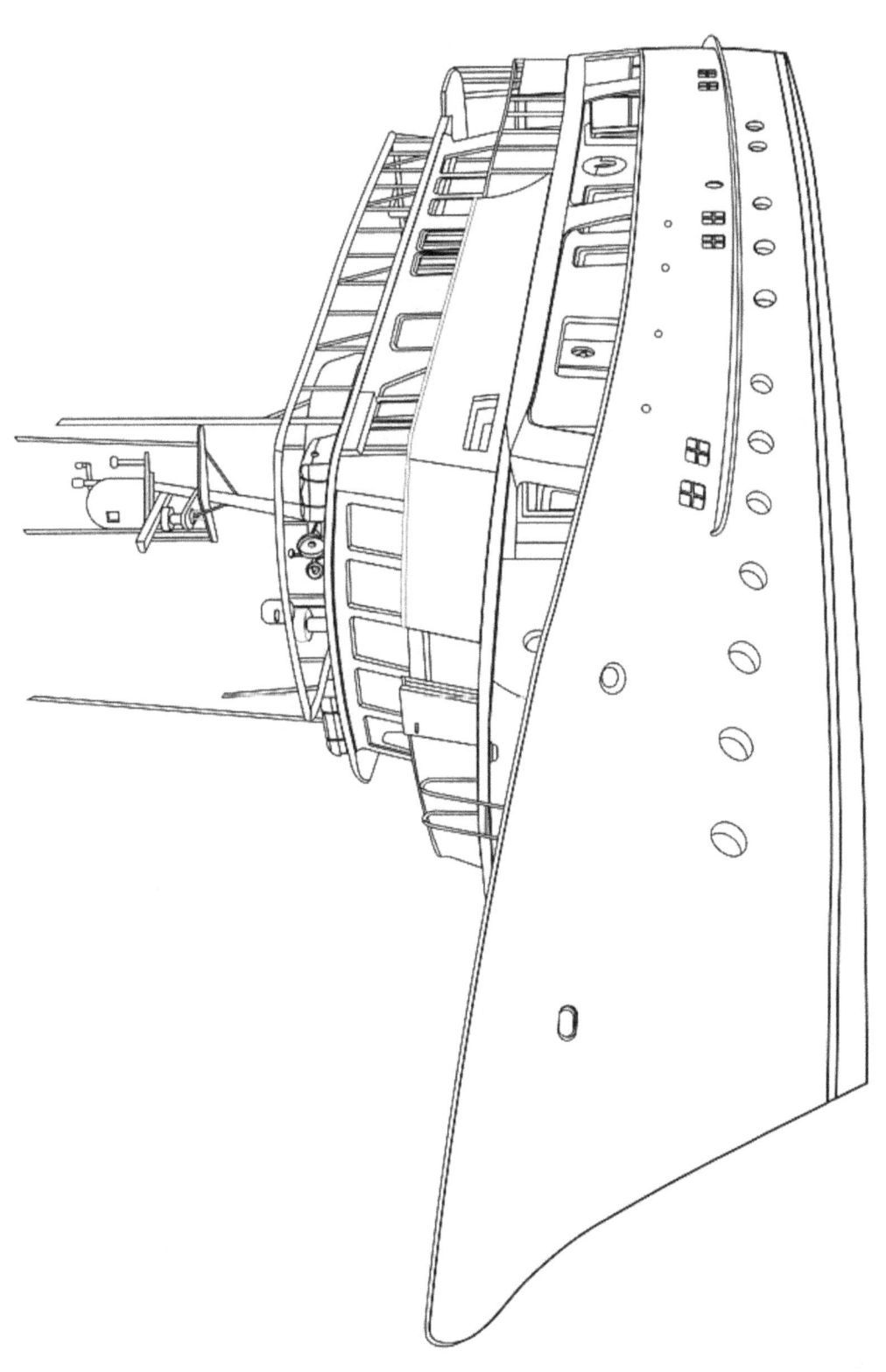

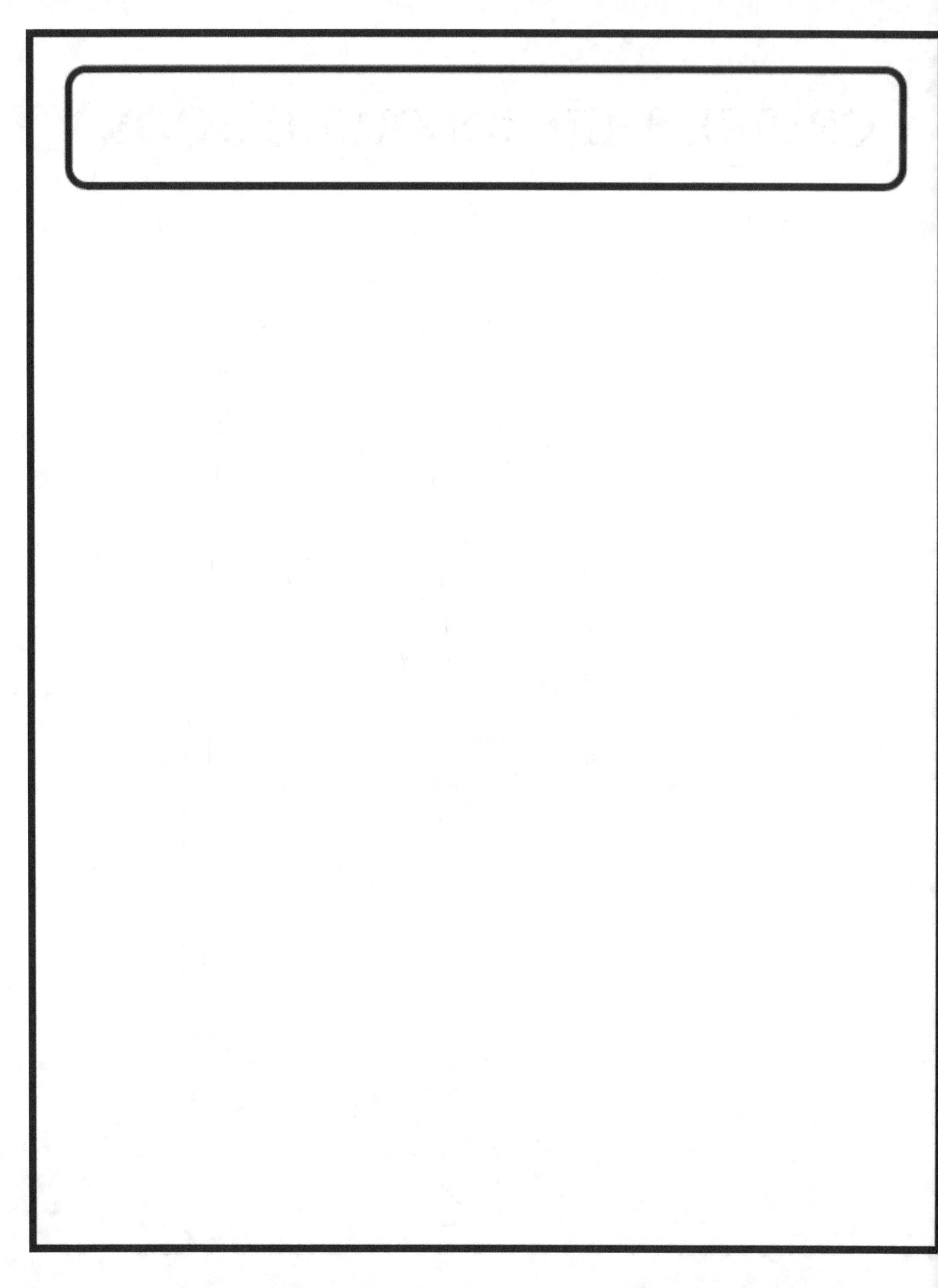

# CRUISE SHIP COLORING BOOK

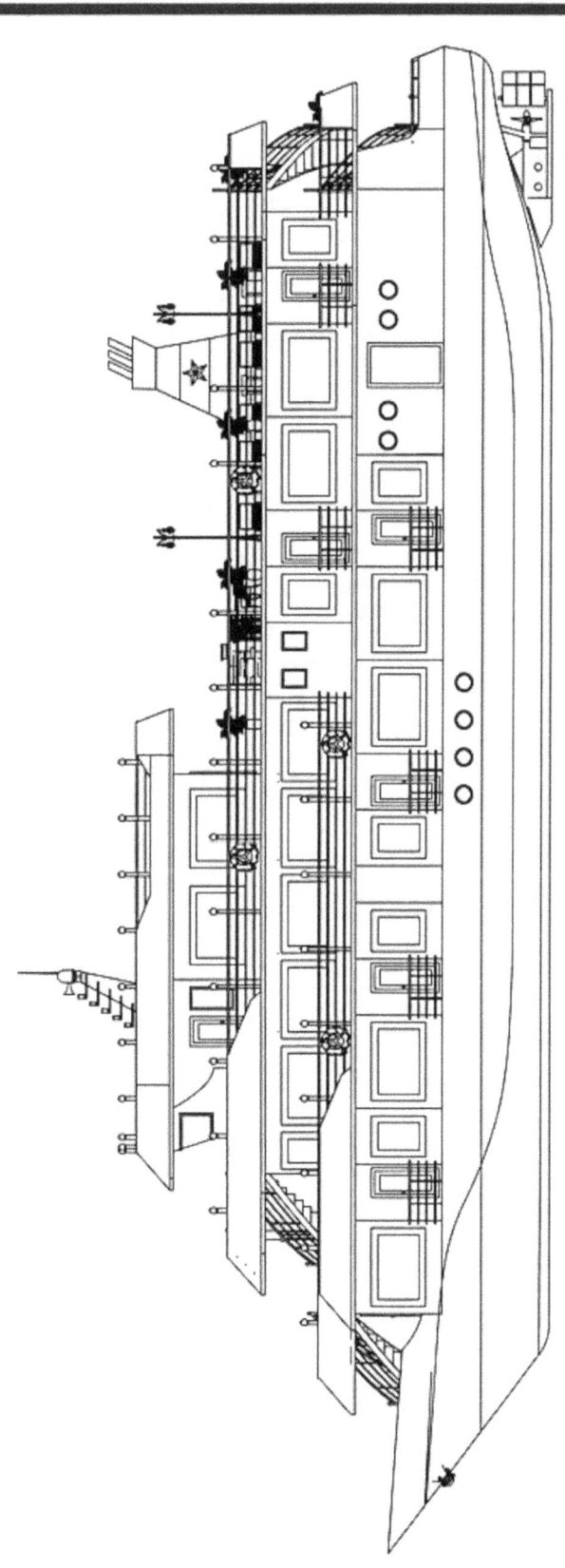

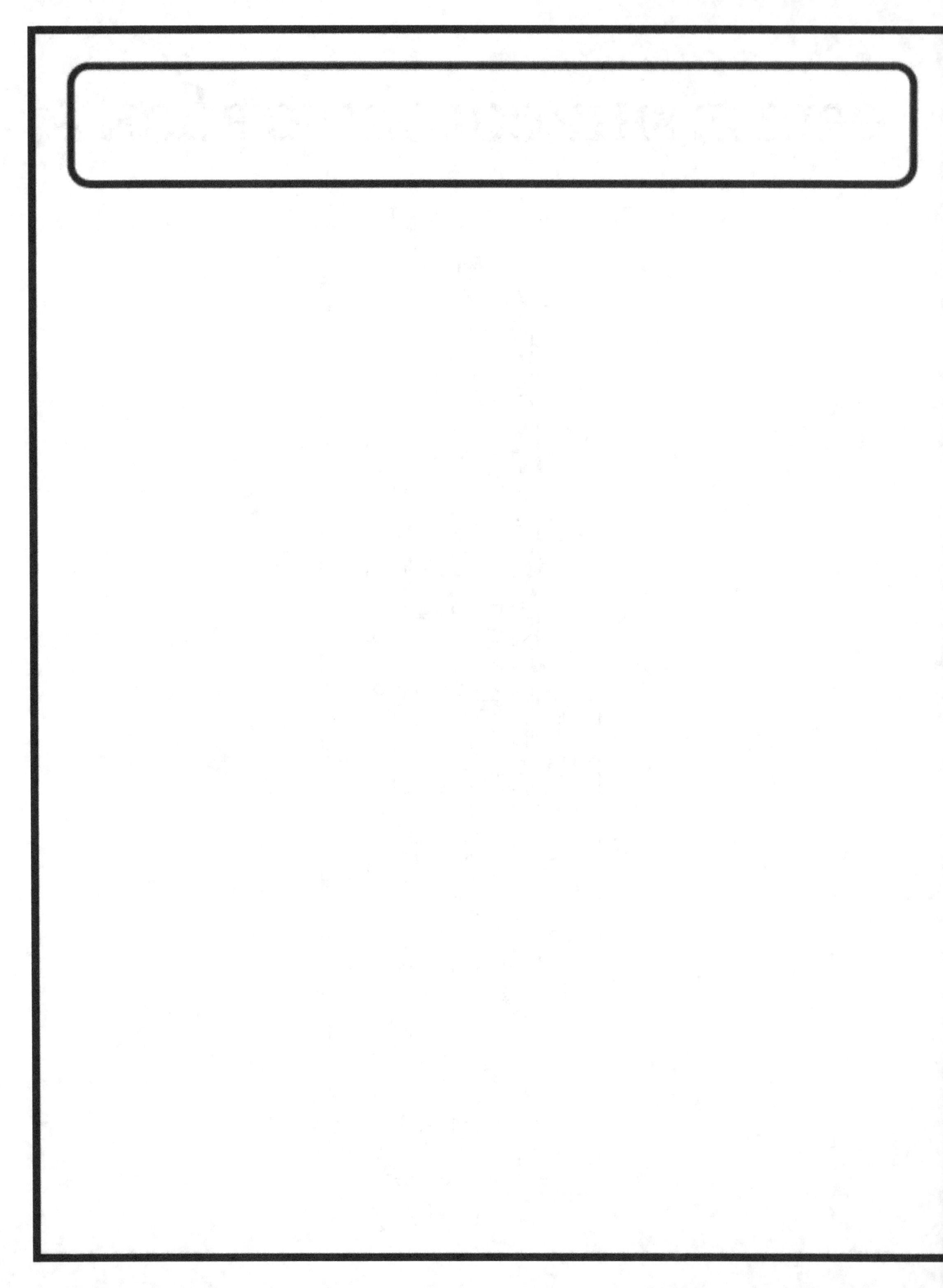

# CRUISE SHIP COLORING BOOK

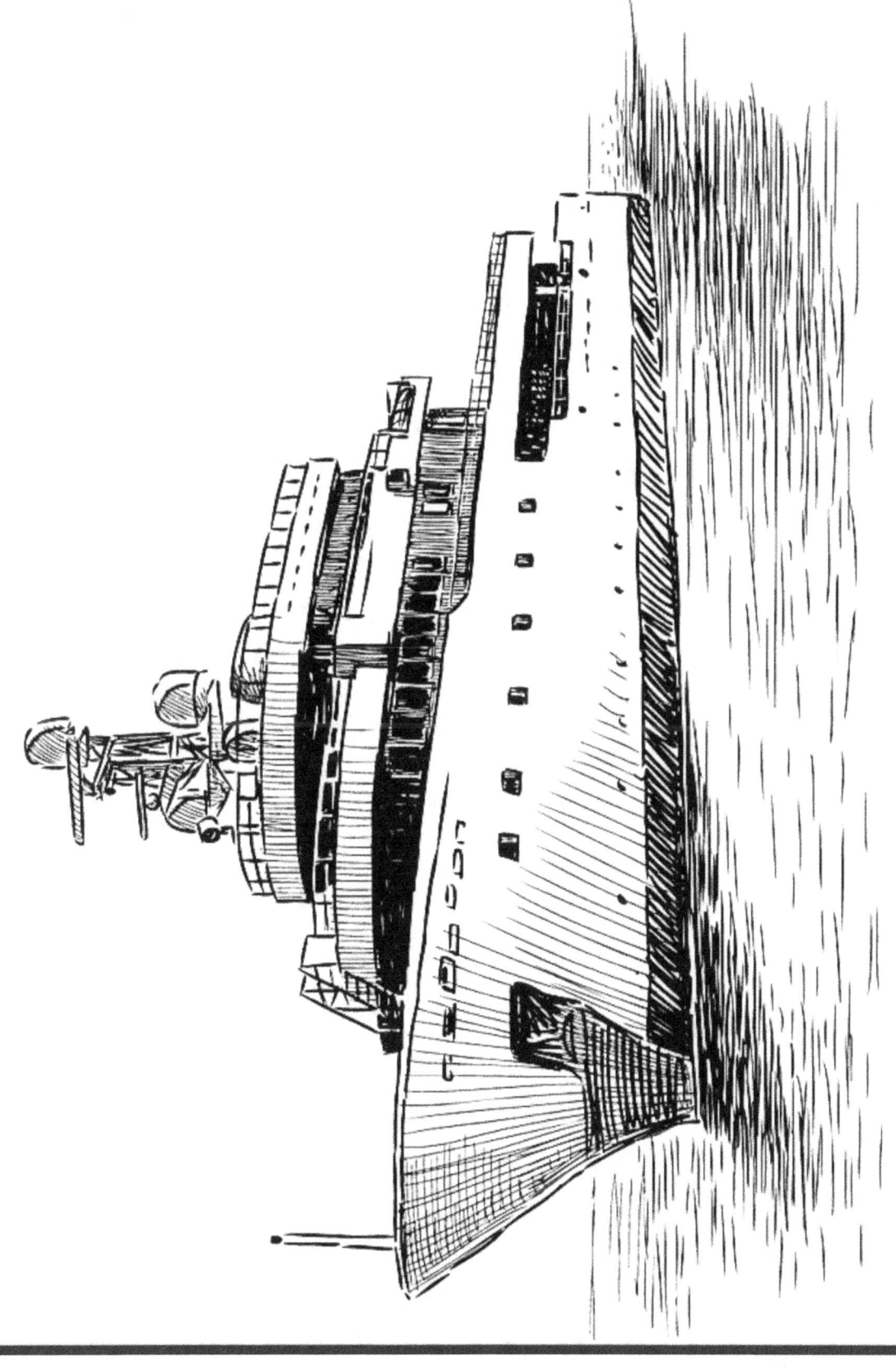

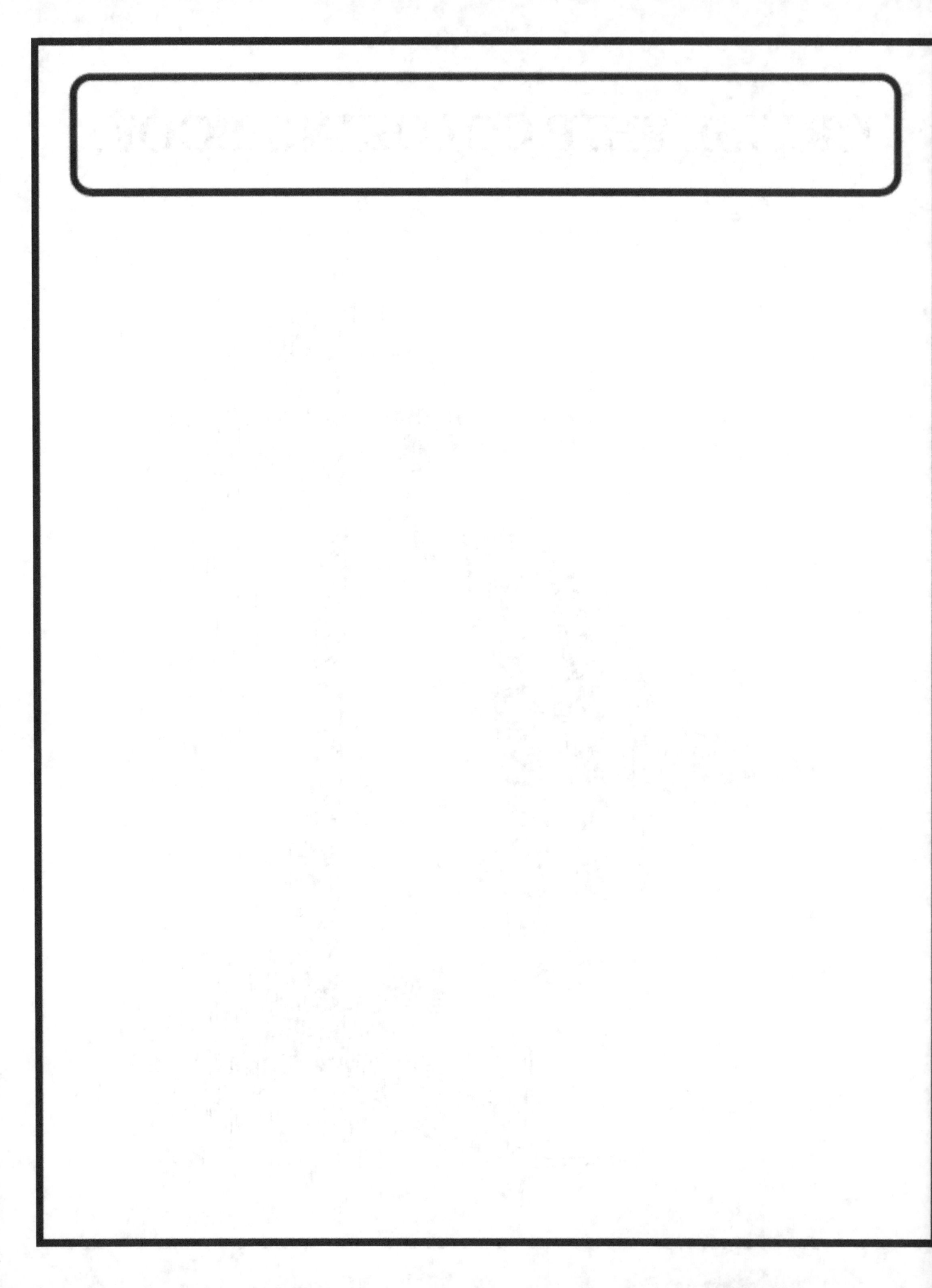

# CRUISE SHIP COLORING BOOK

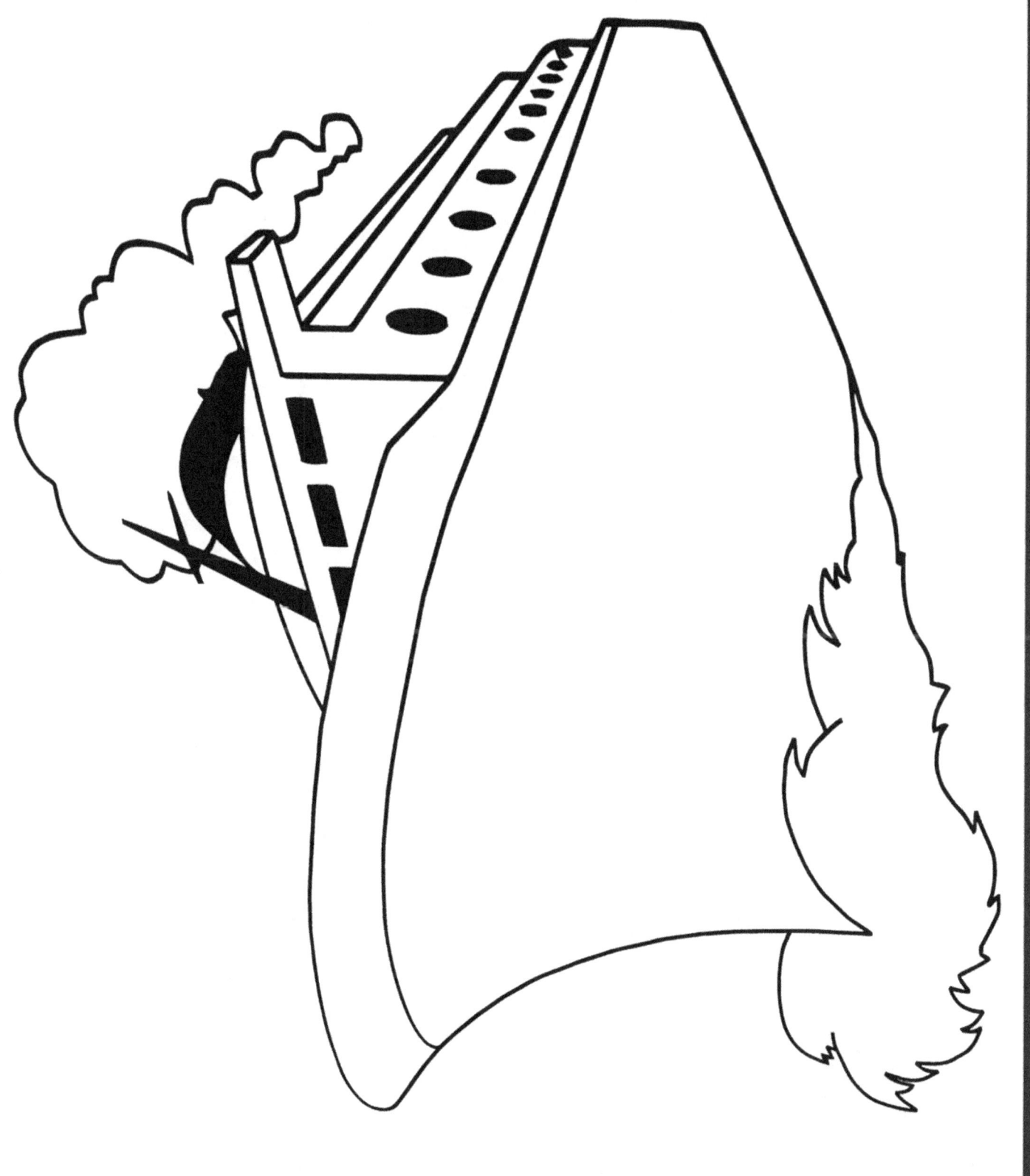

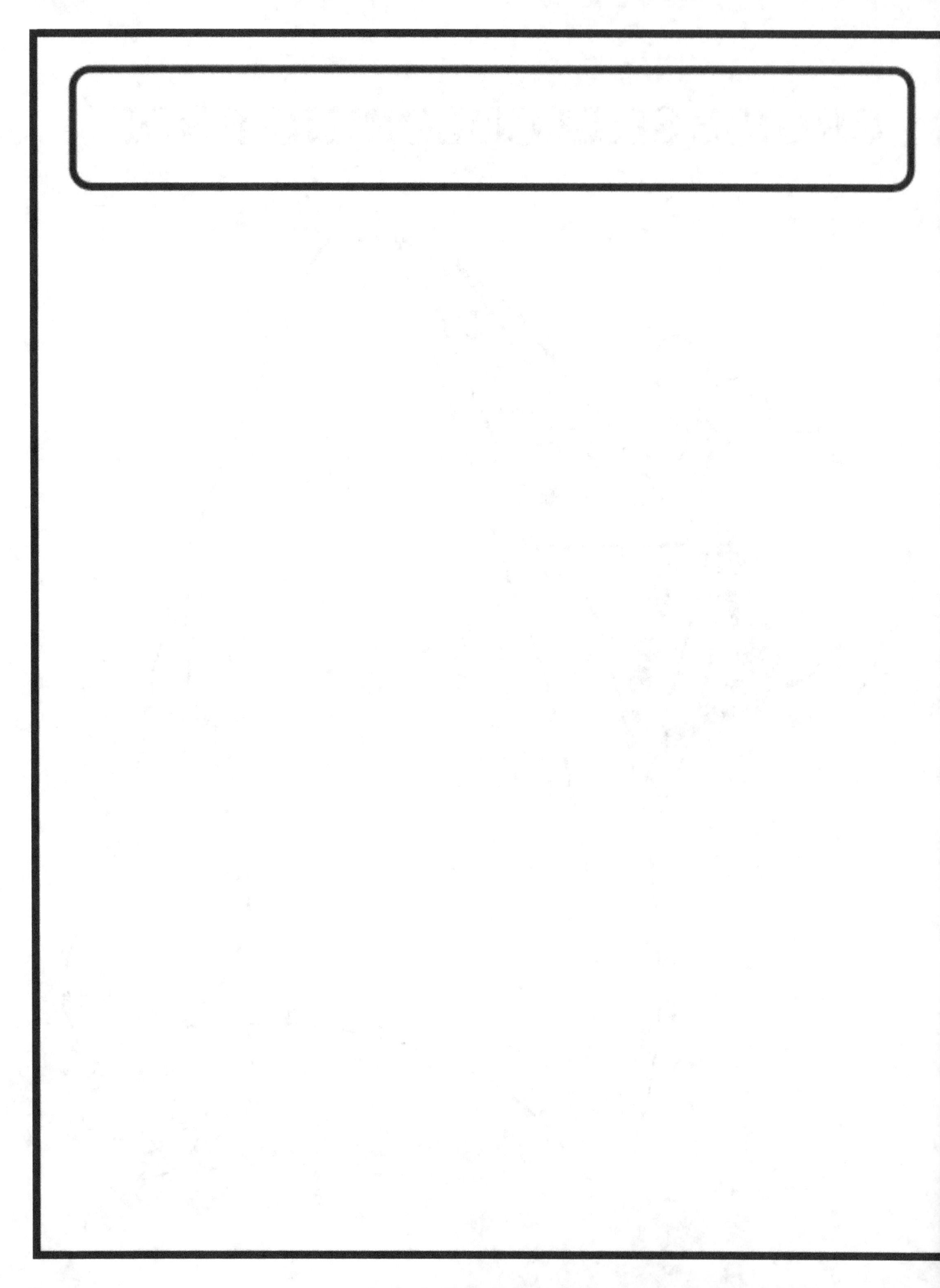

# CRUISE SHIP COLORING BOOK

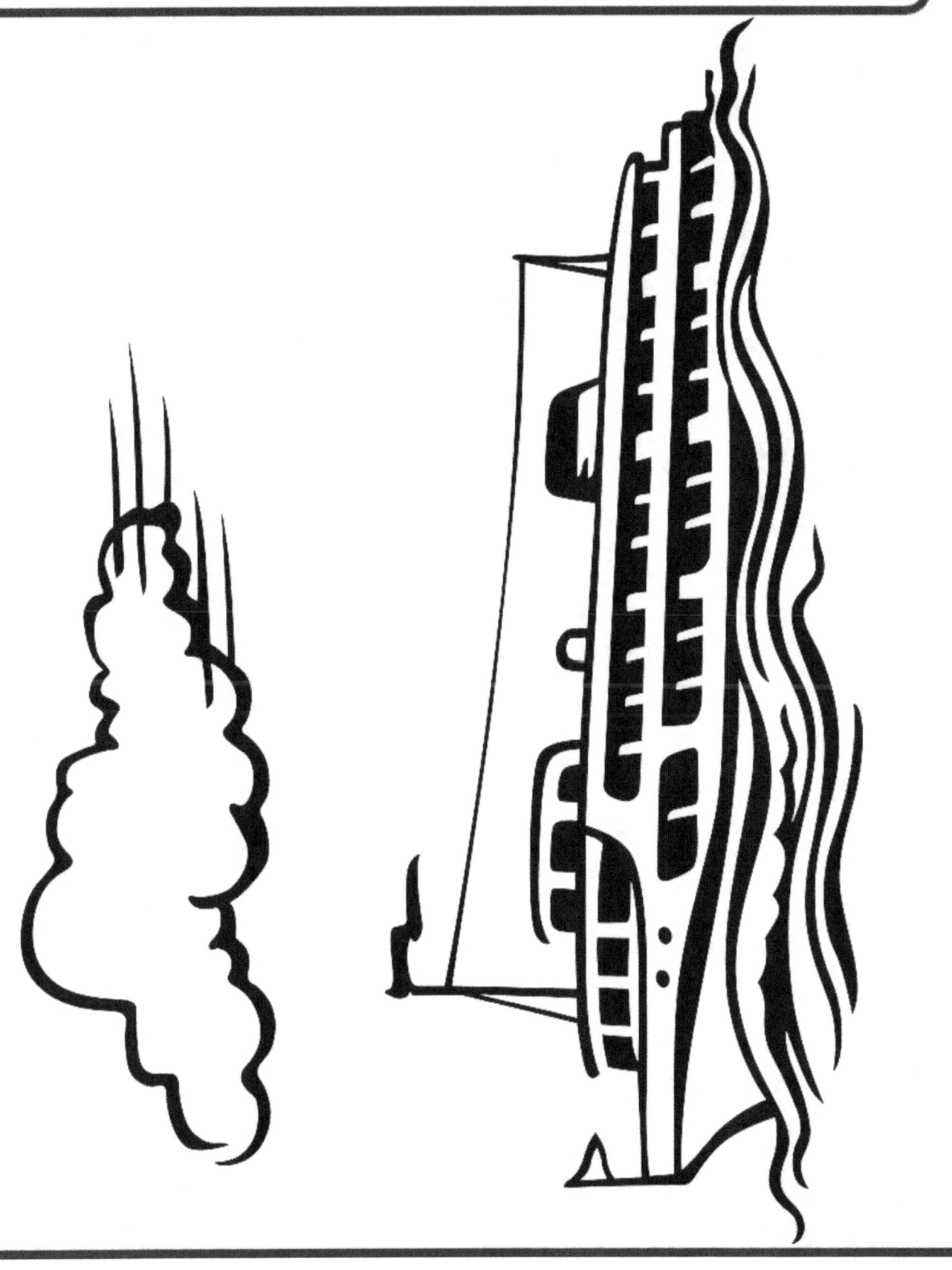

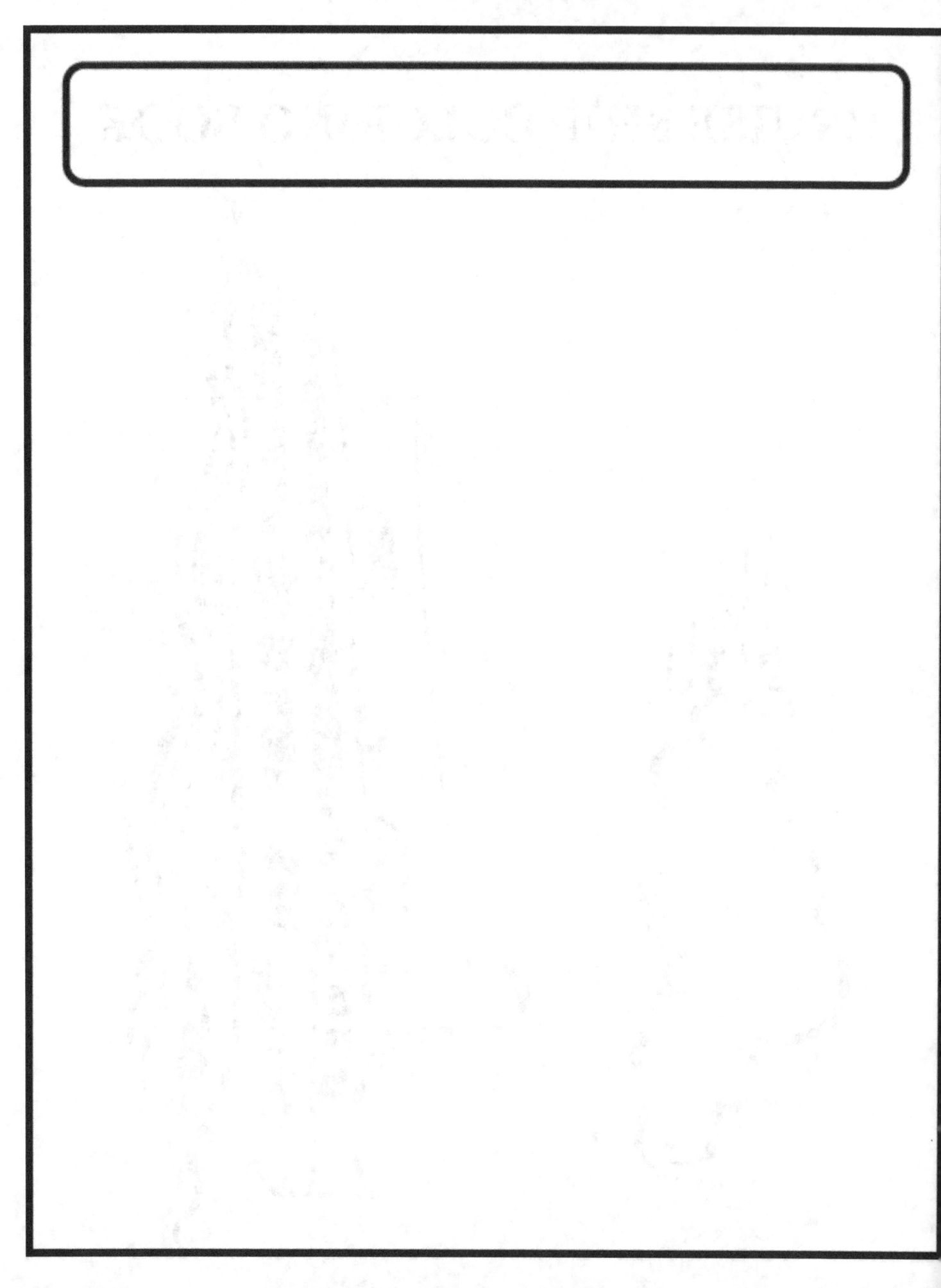

# CRUISE SHIP COLORING BOOK

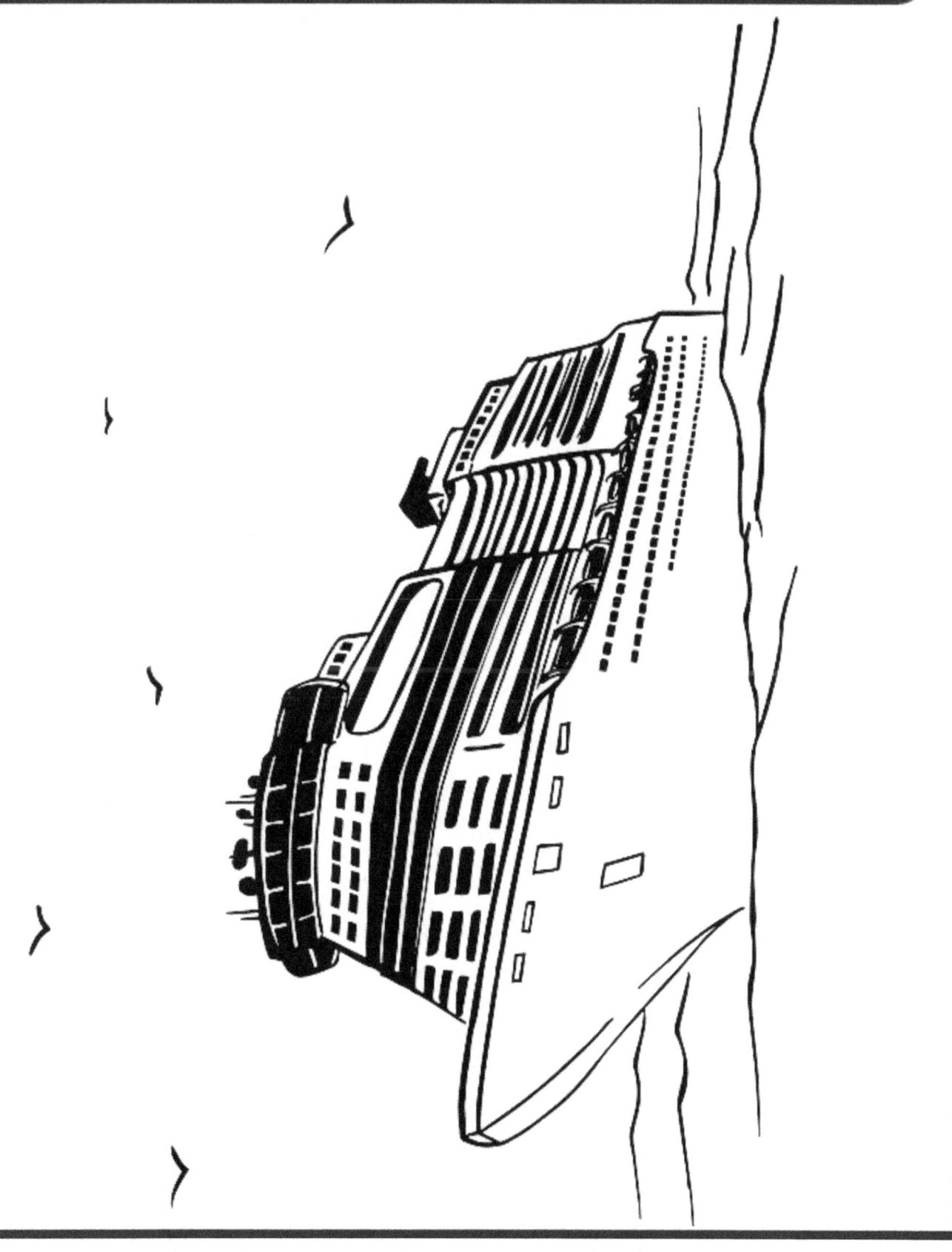

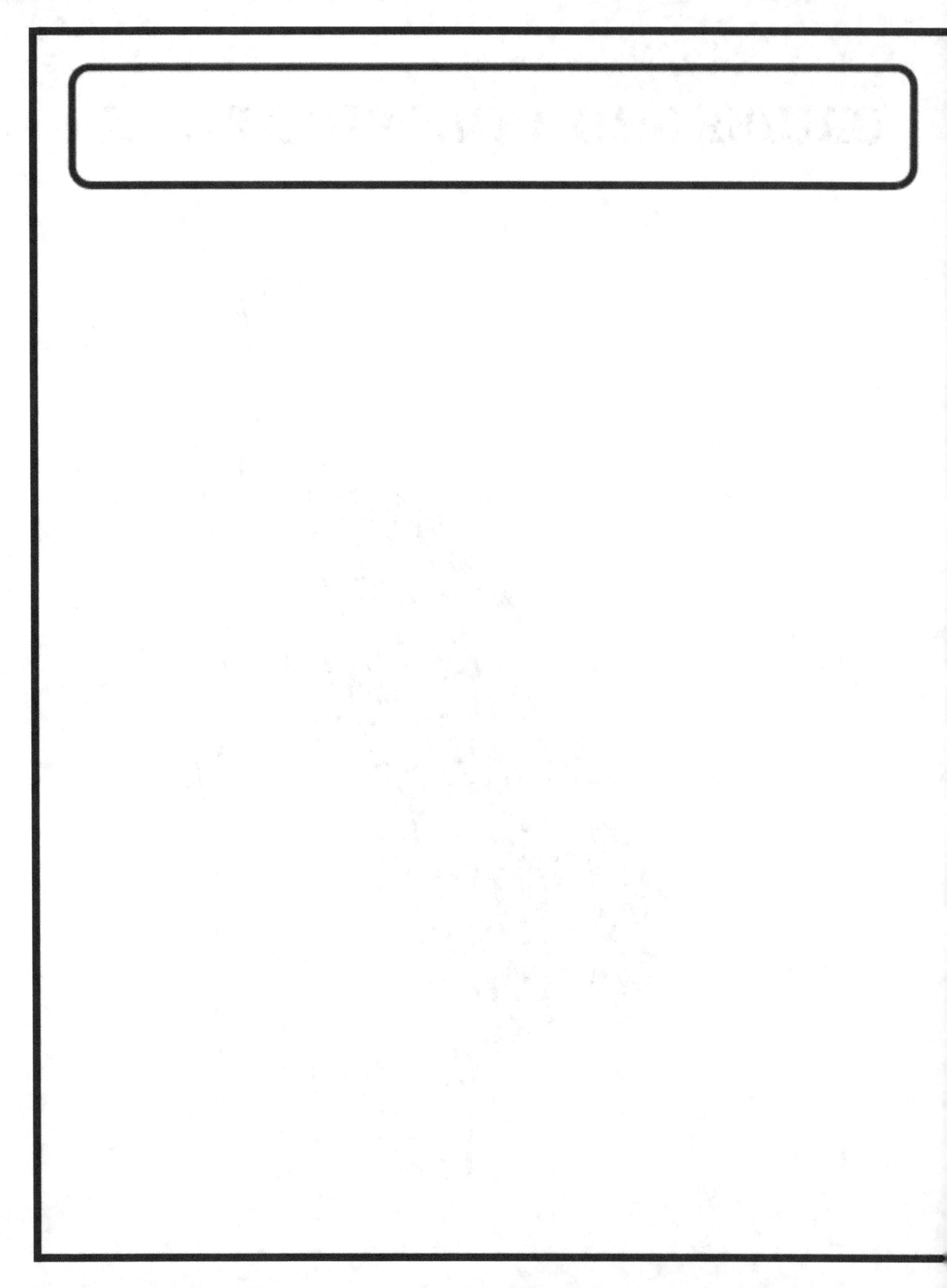

# CRUISE SHIP COLORING BOOK

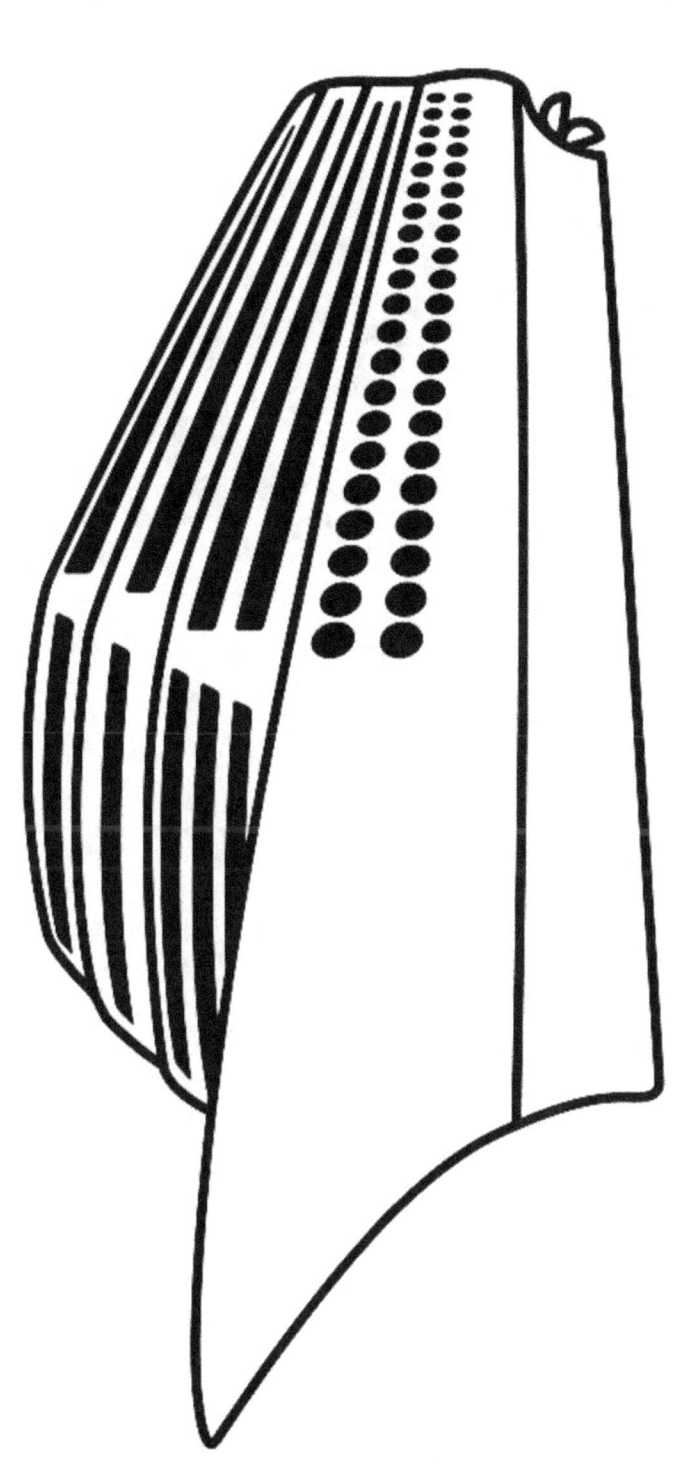

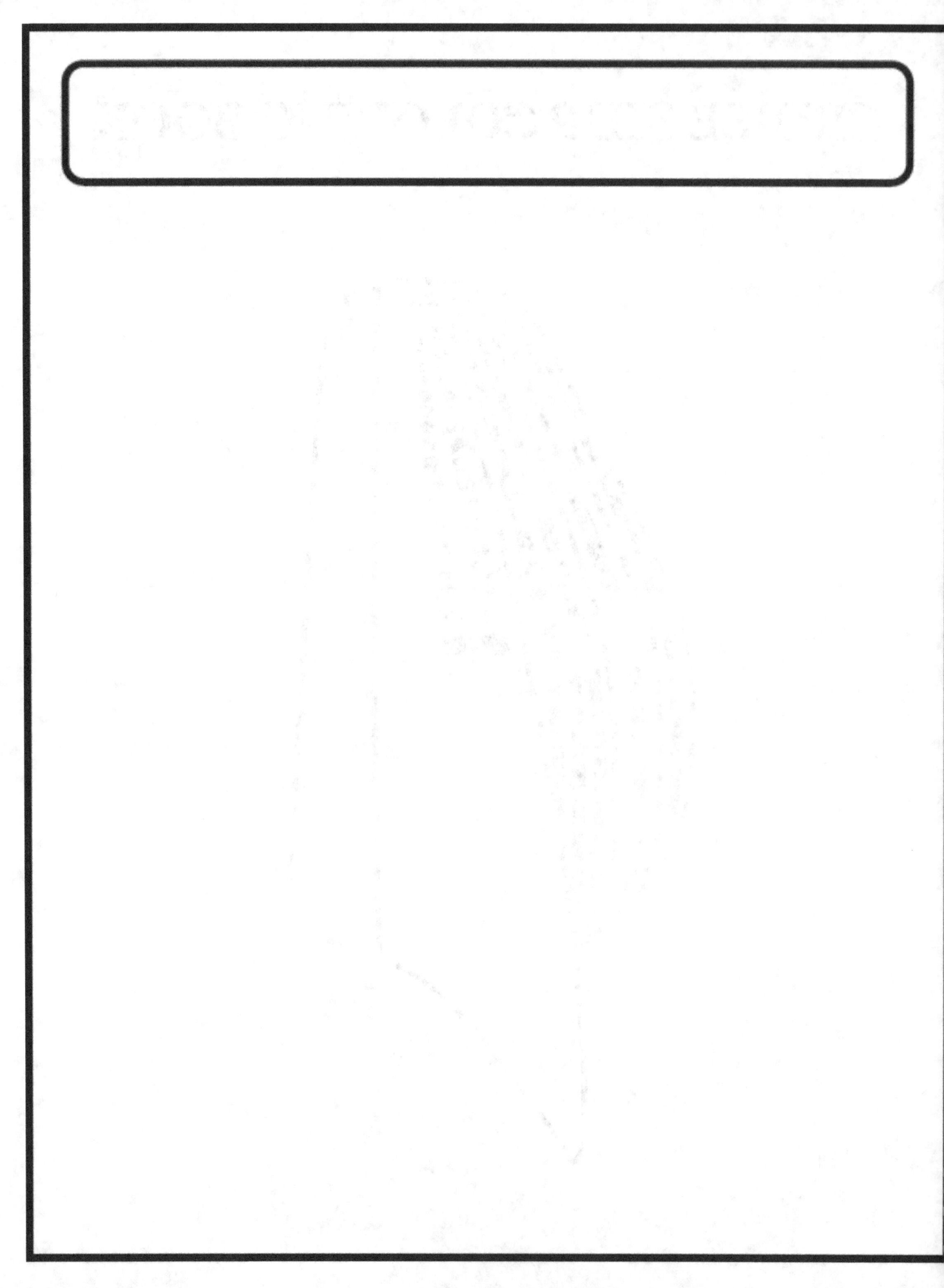

# CRUISE SHIP COLORING BOOK

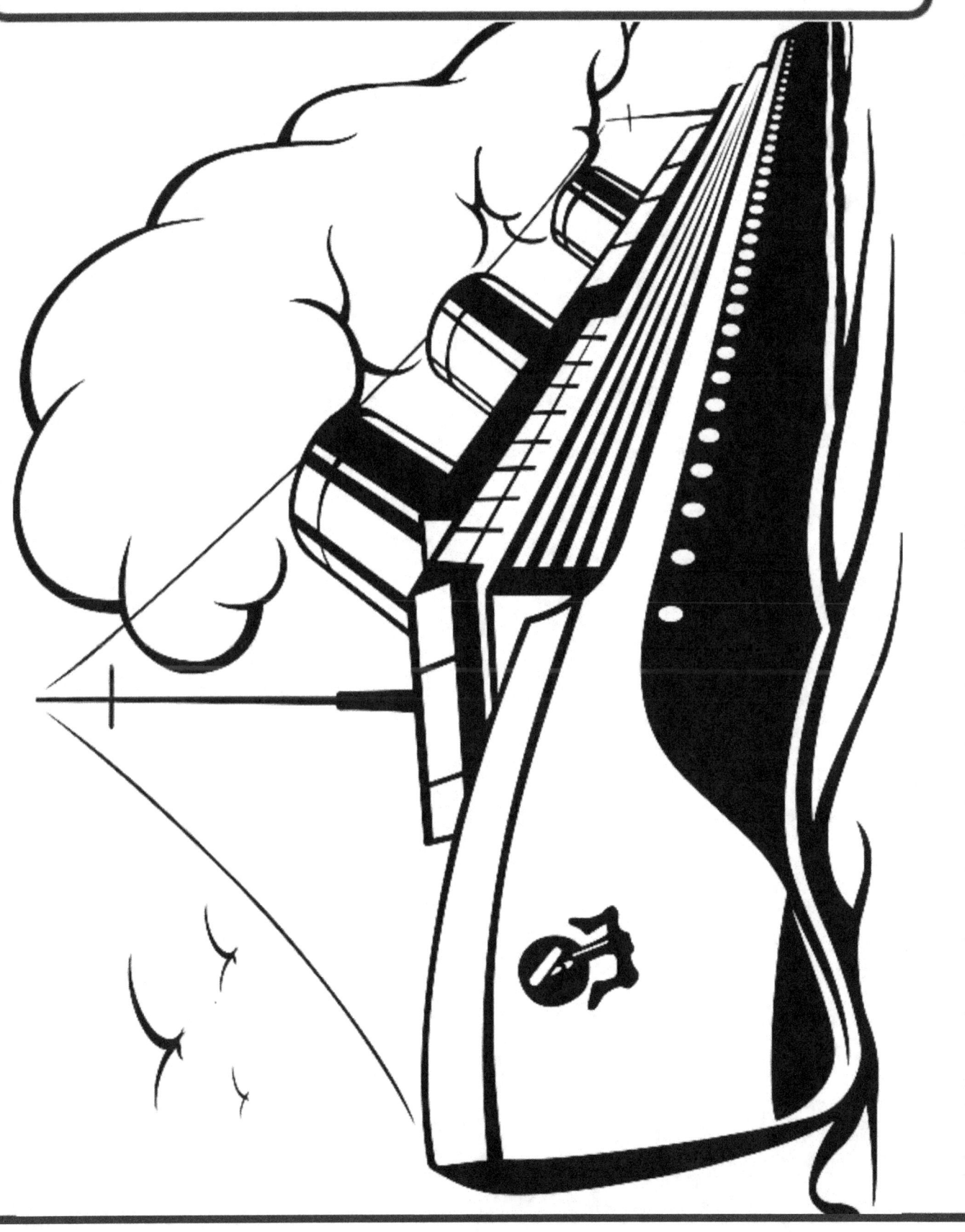

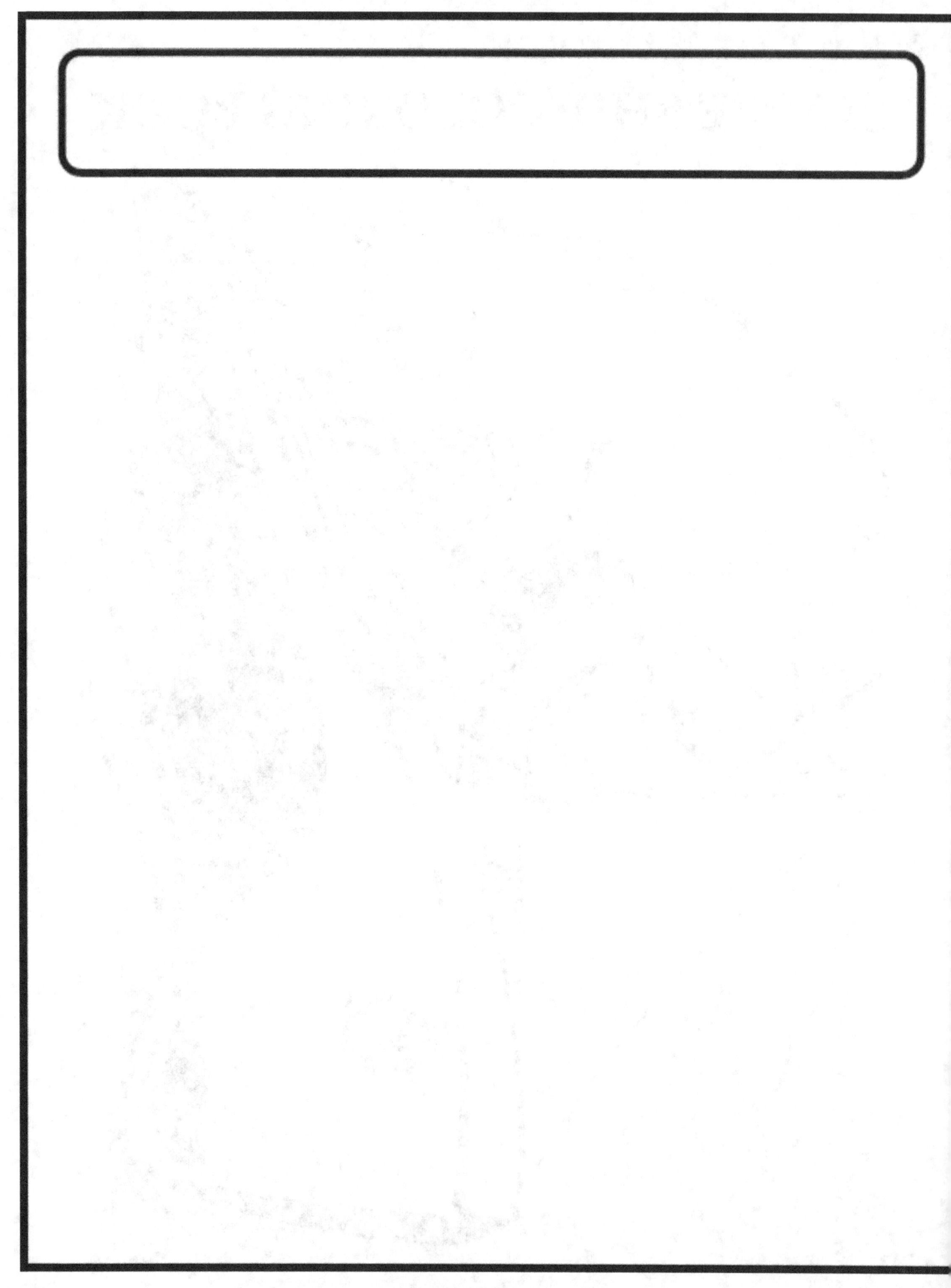

# CRUISE SHIP COLORING BOOK

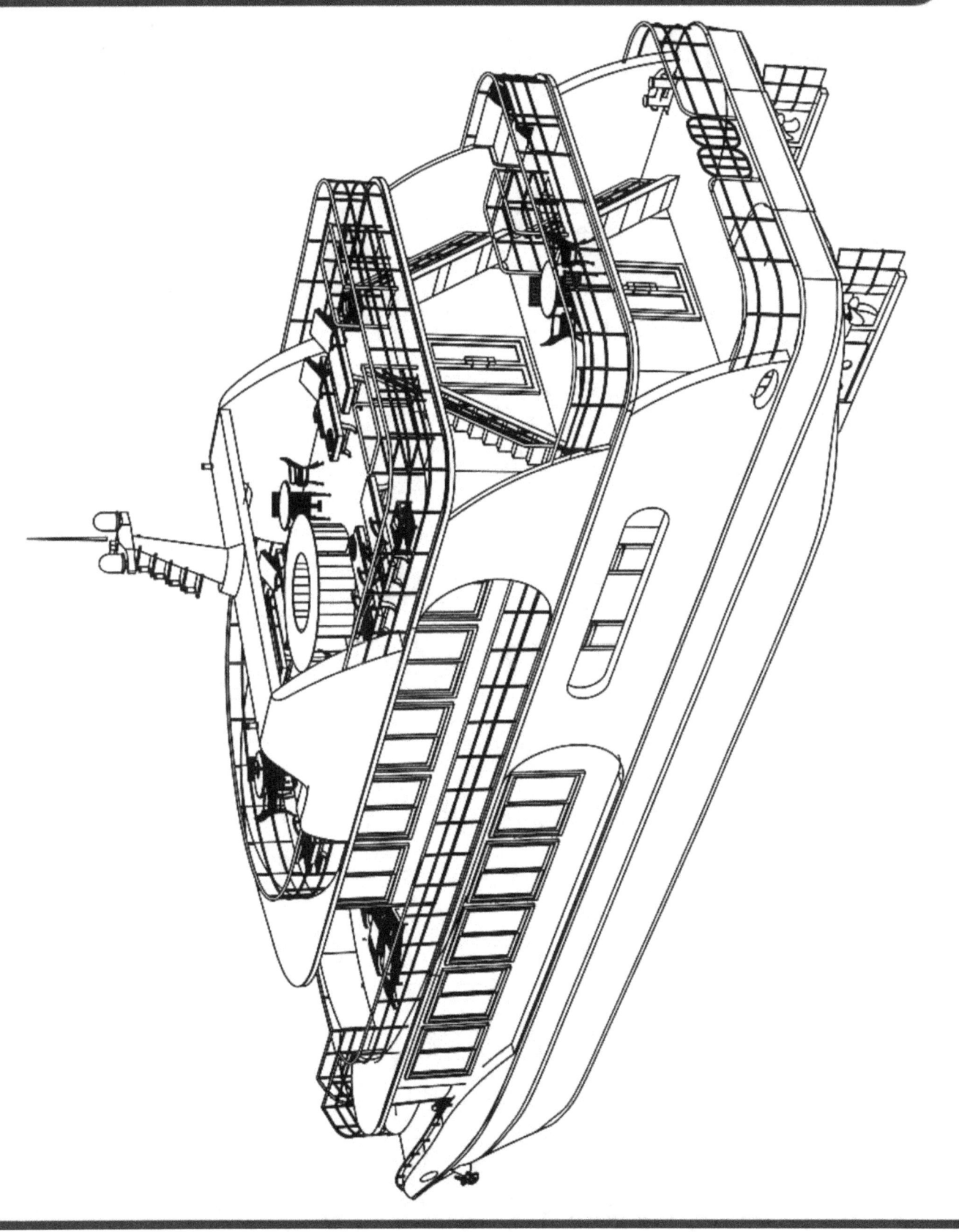

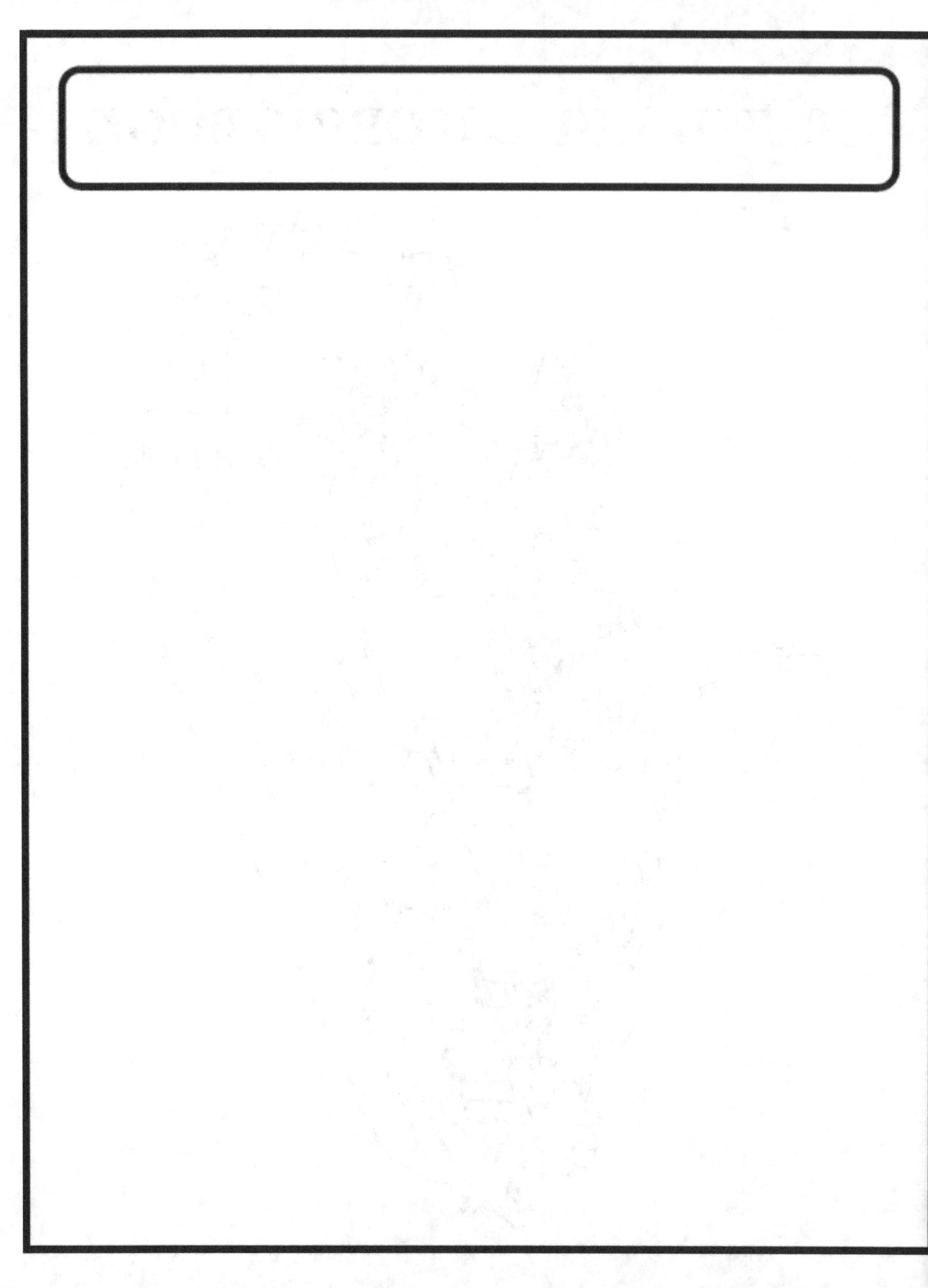

# CRUISE SHIP COLORING BOOK

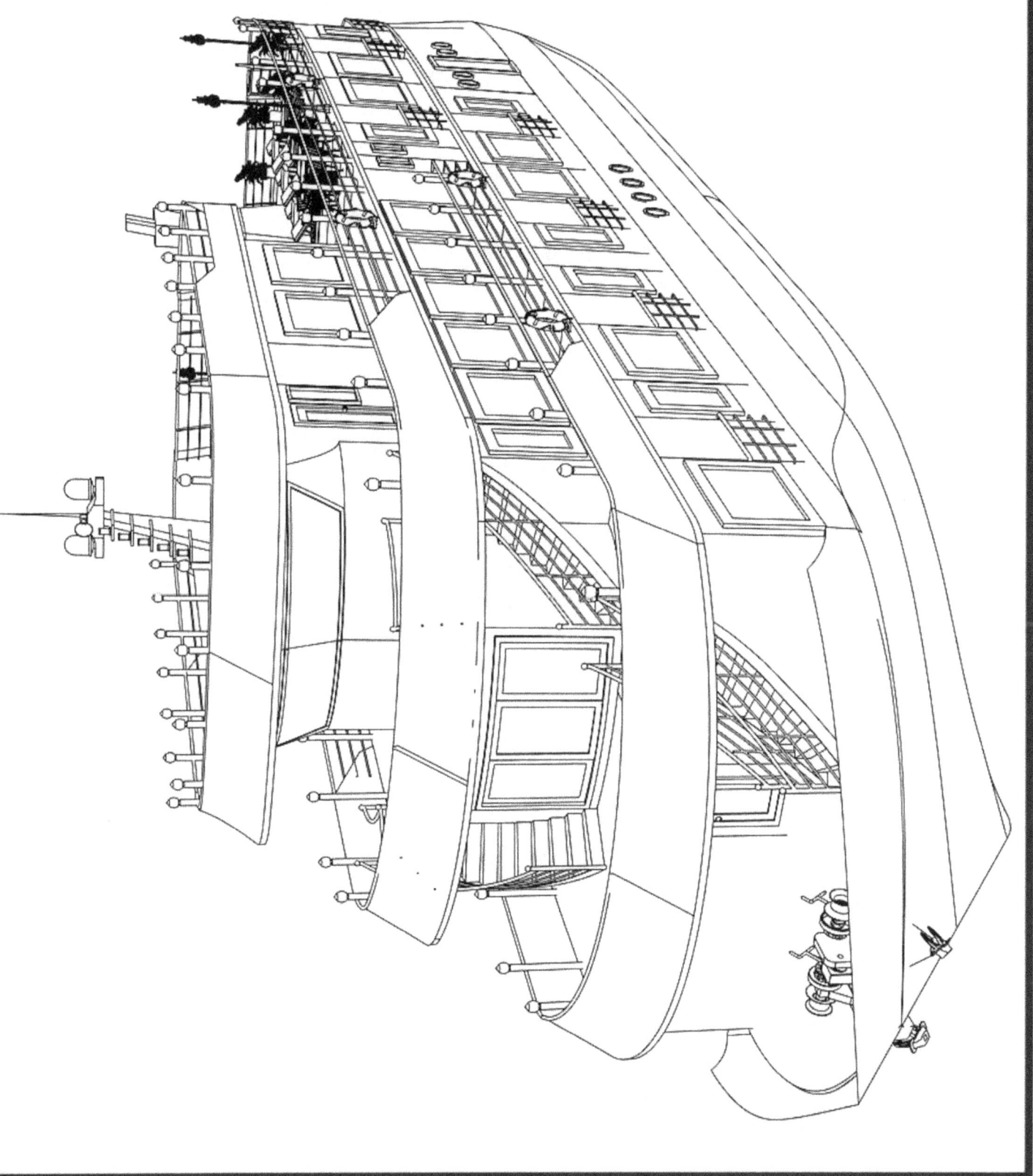

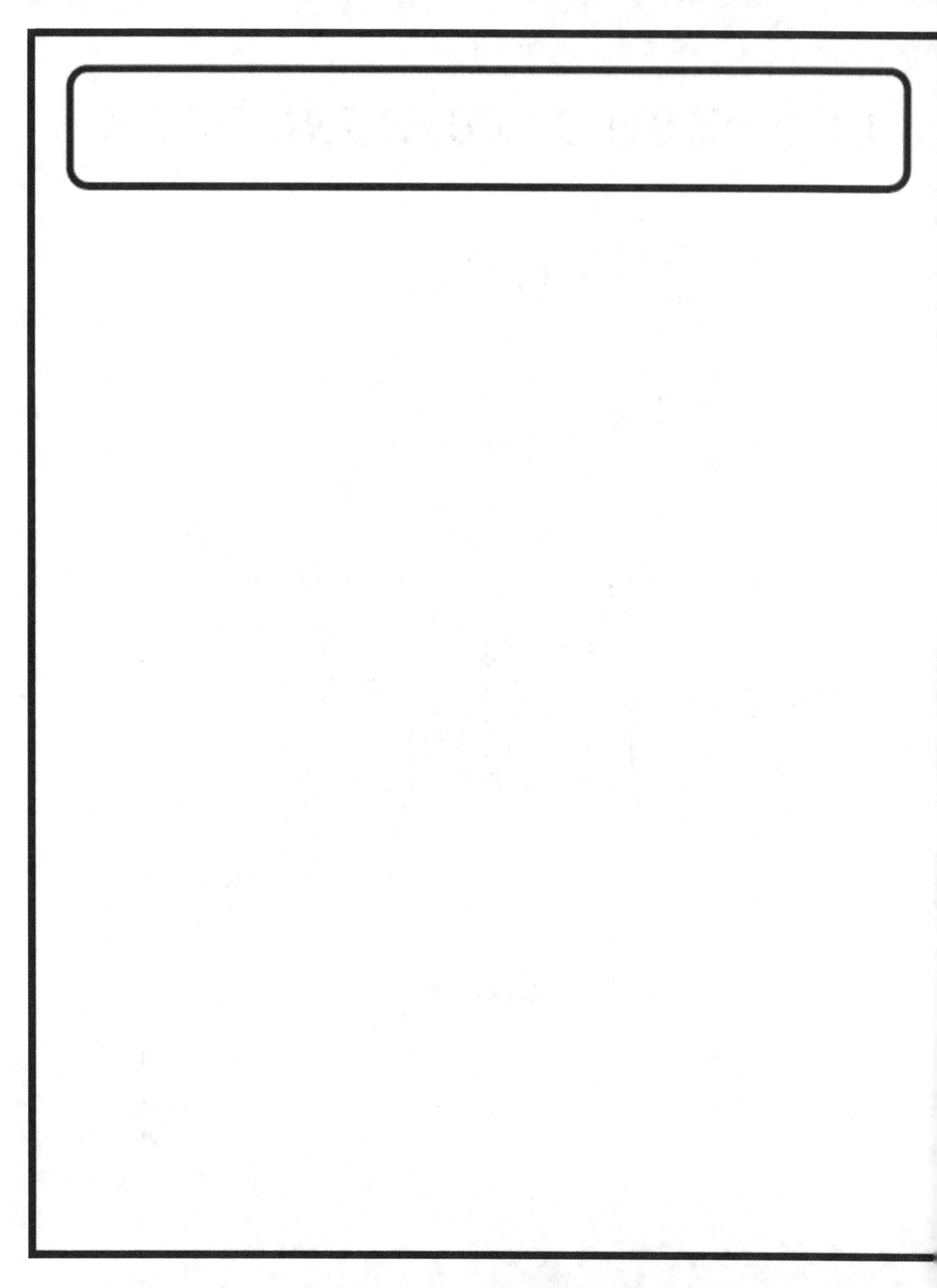

# CRUISE SHIP COLORING BOOK

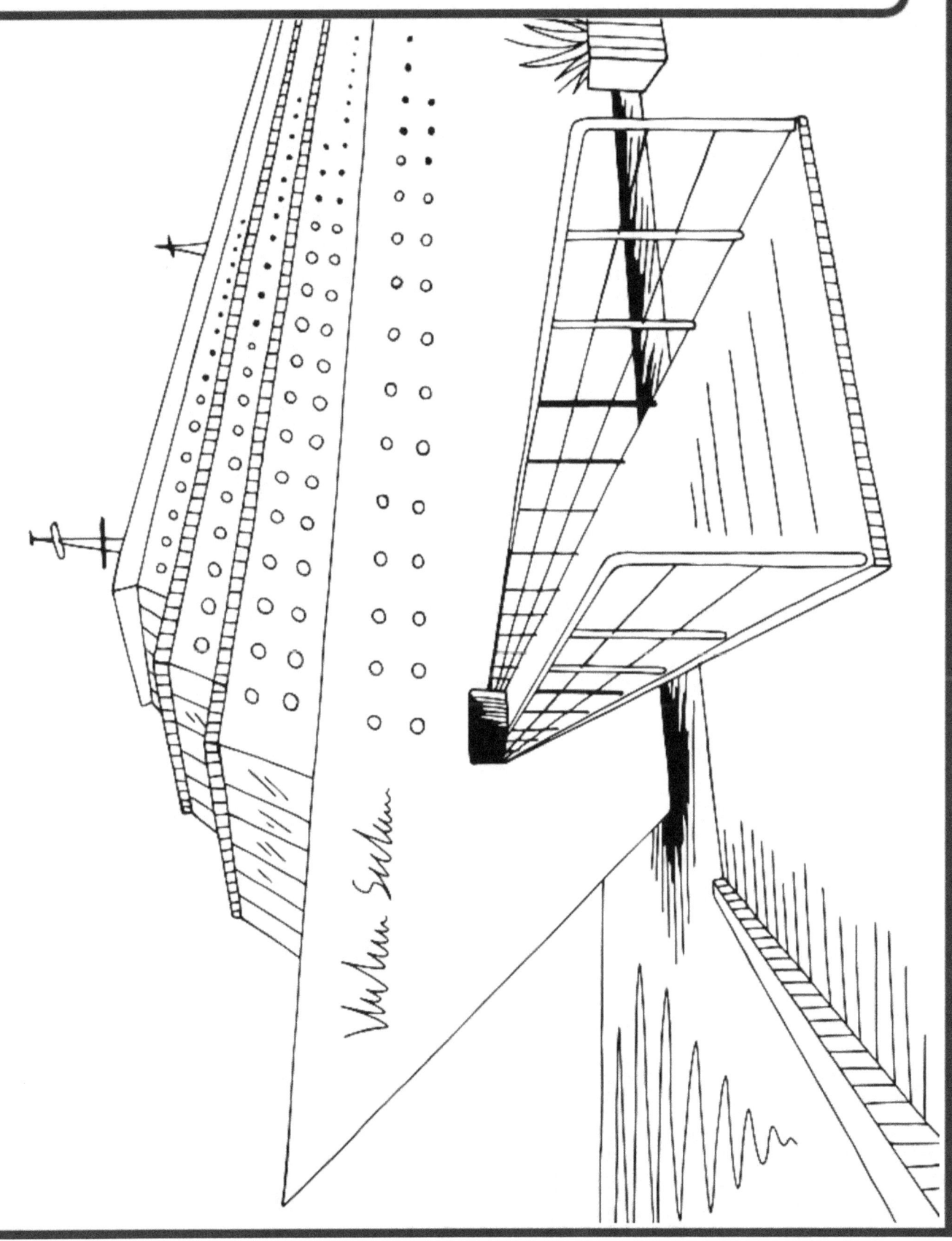

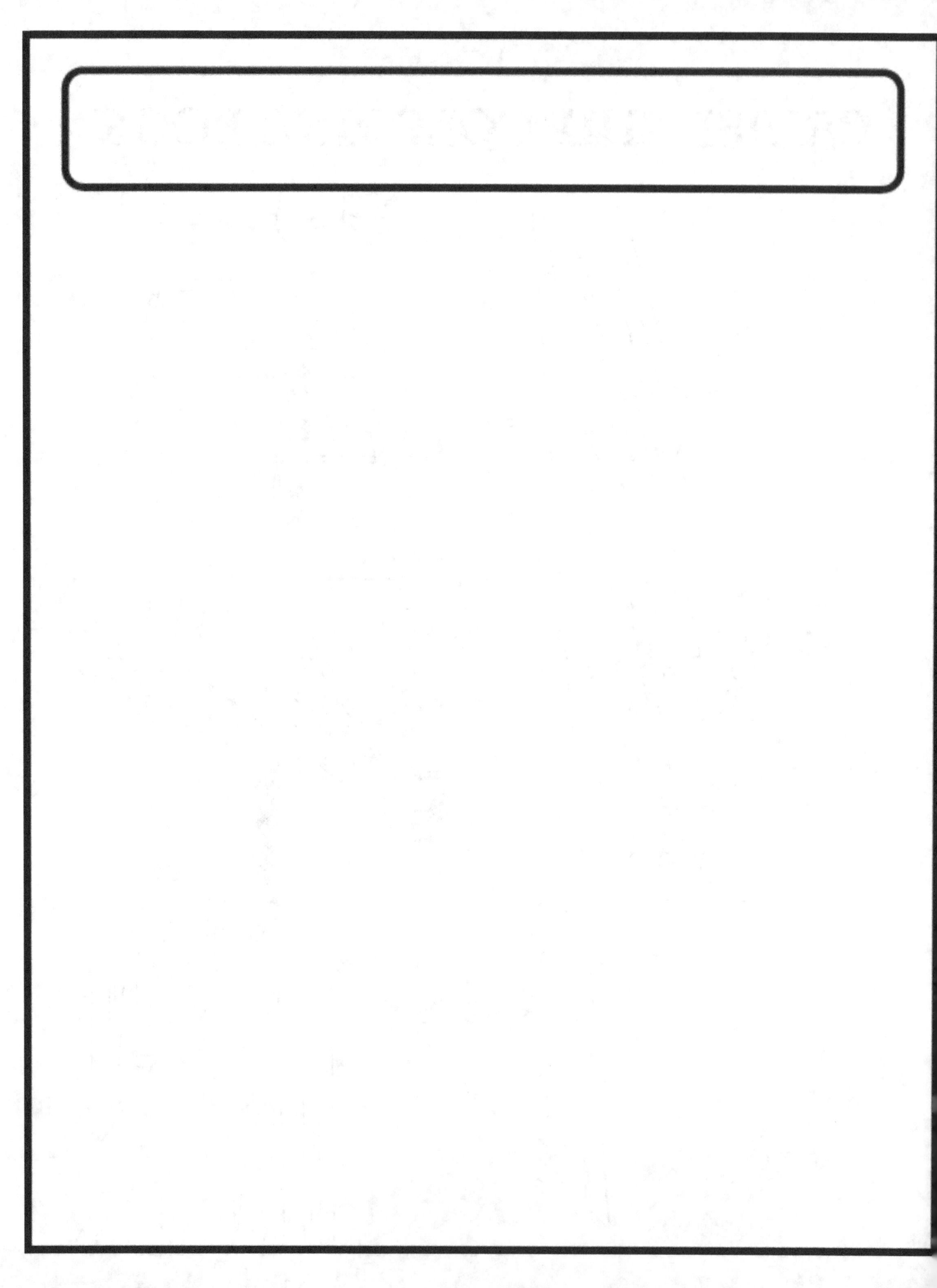

# CRUISE SHIP COLORING BOOK

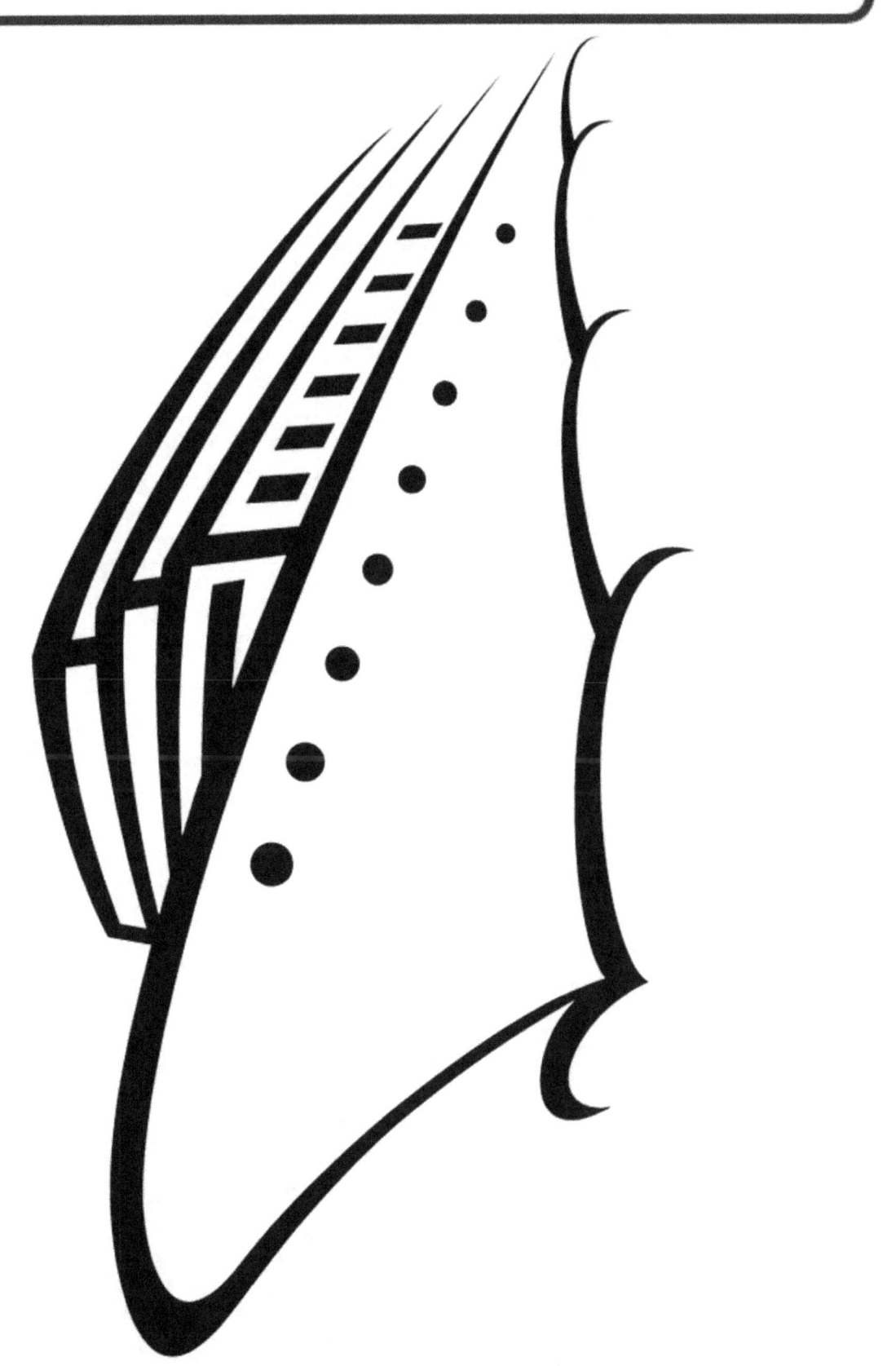

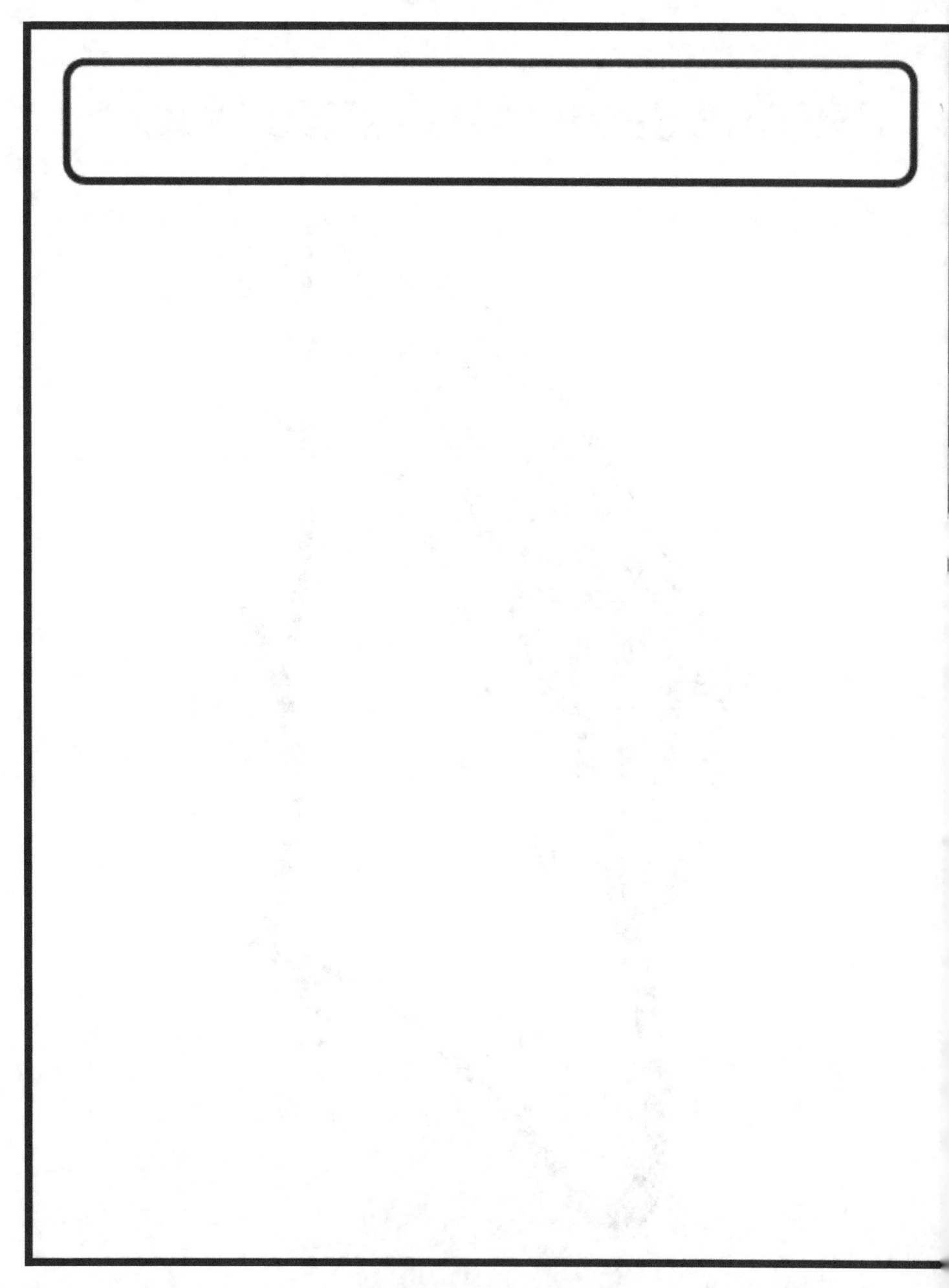

# CRUISE SHIP COLORING BOOK

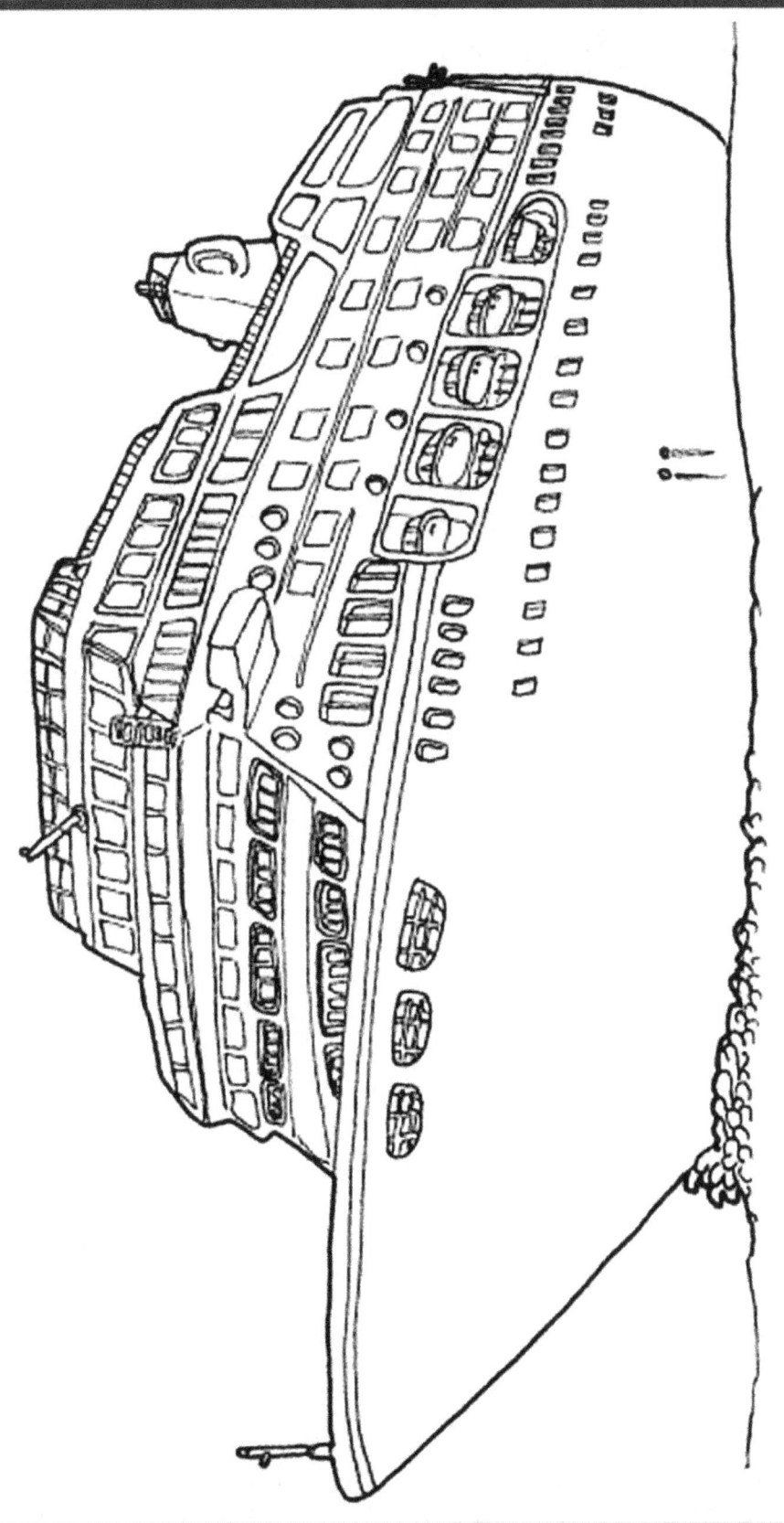

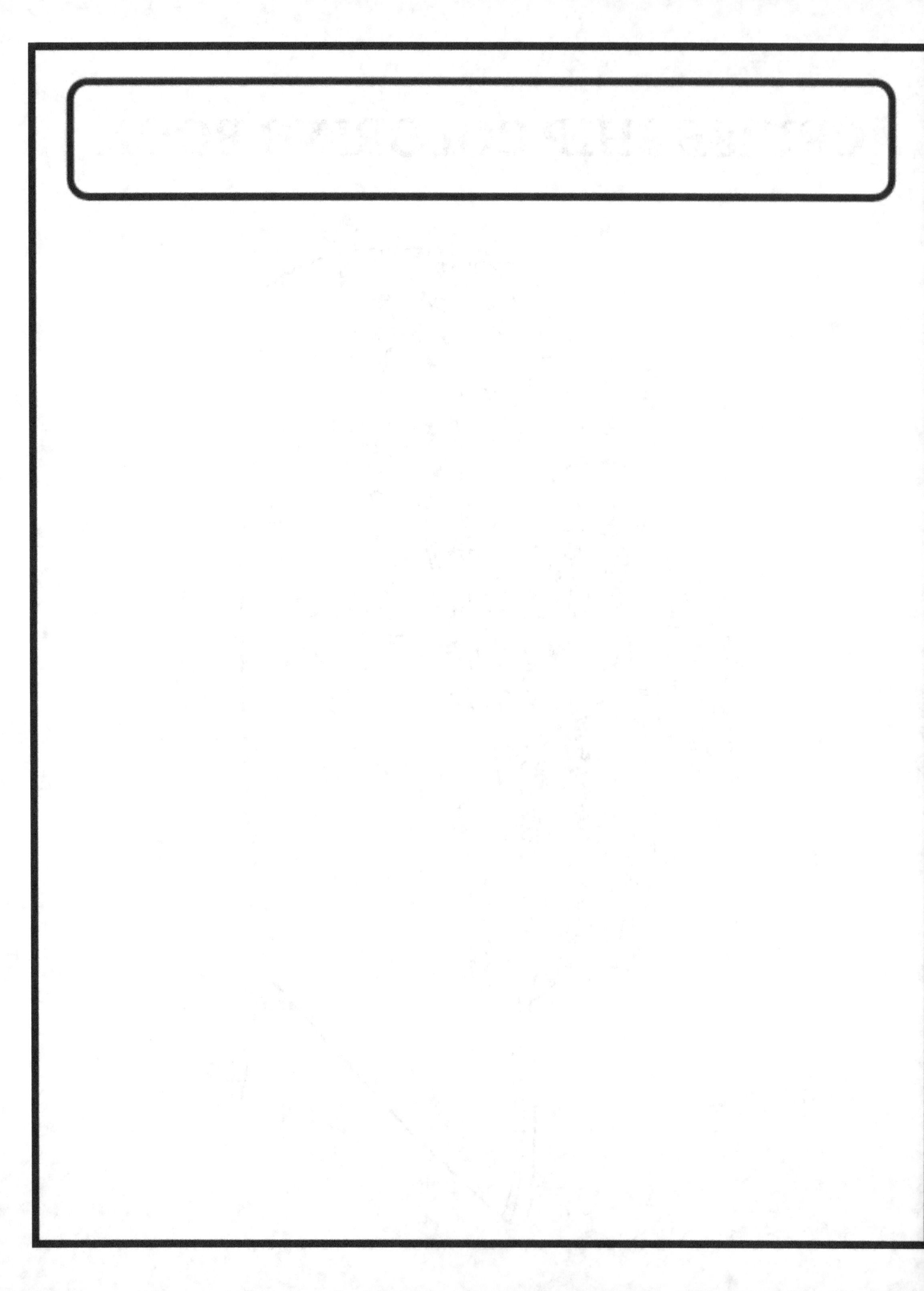

# CRUISE SHIP COLORING BOOK

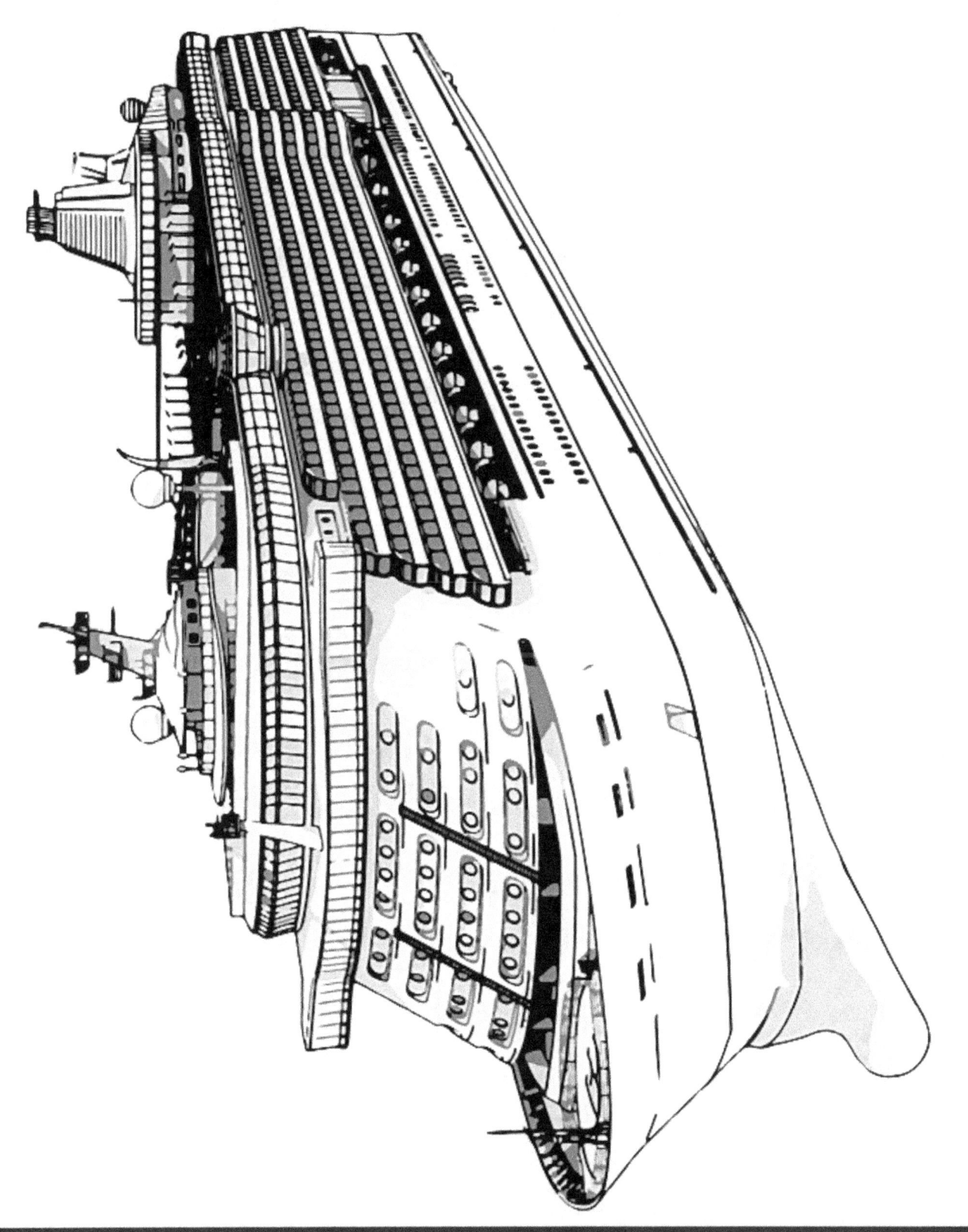

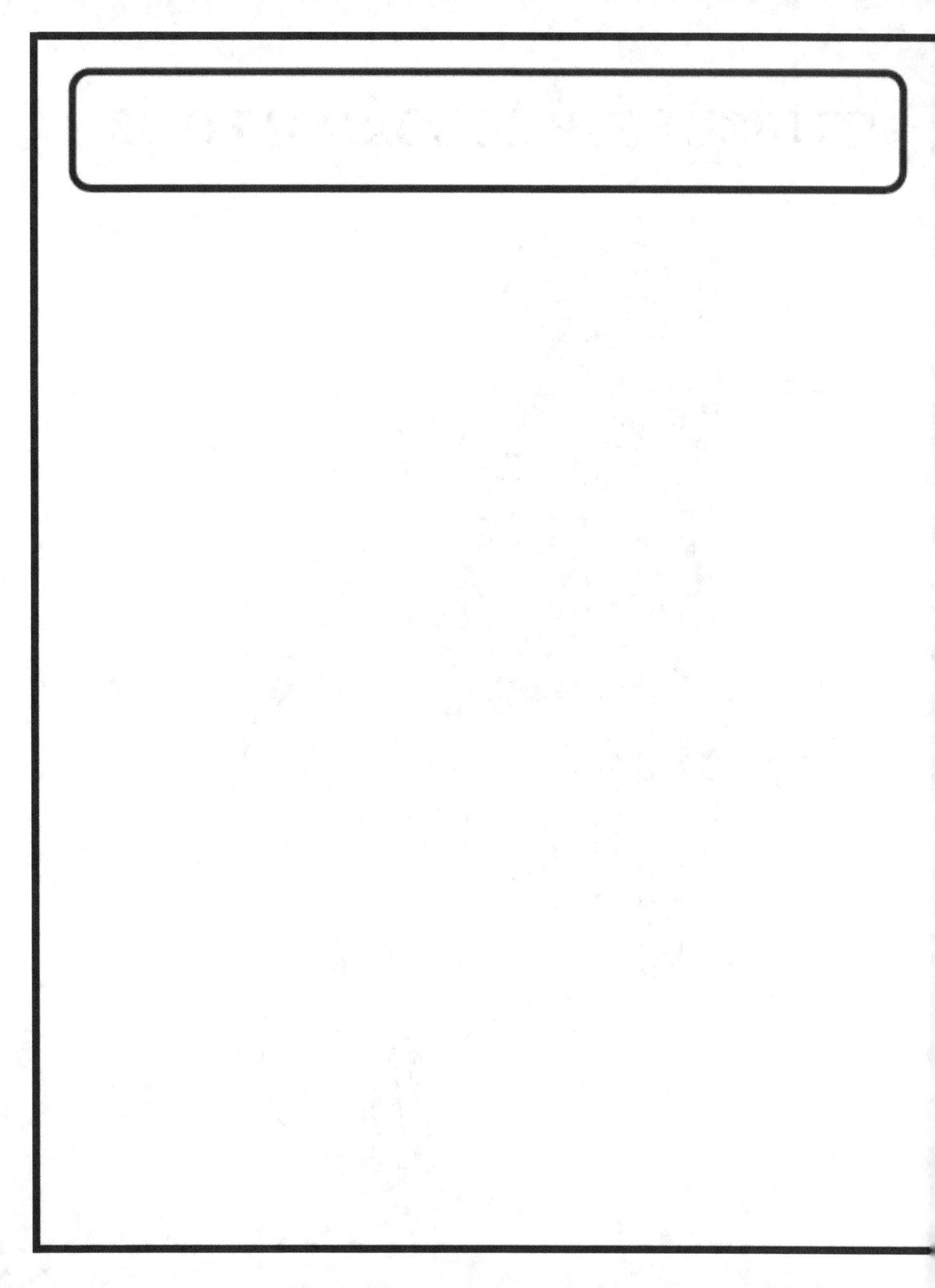

# CRUISE SHIP COLORING BOOK

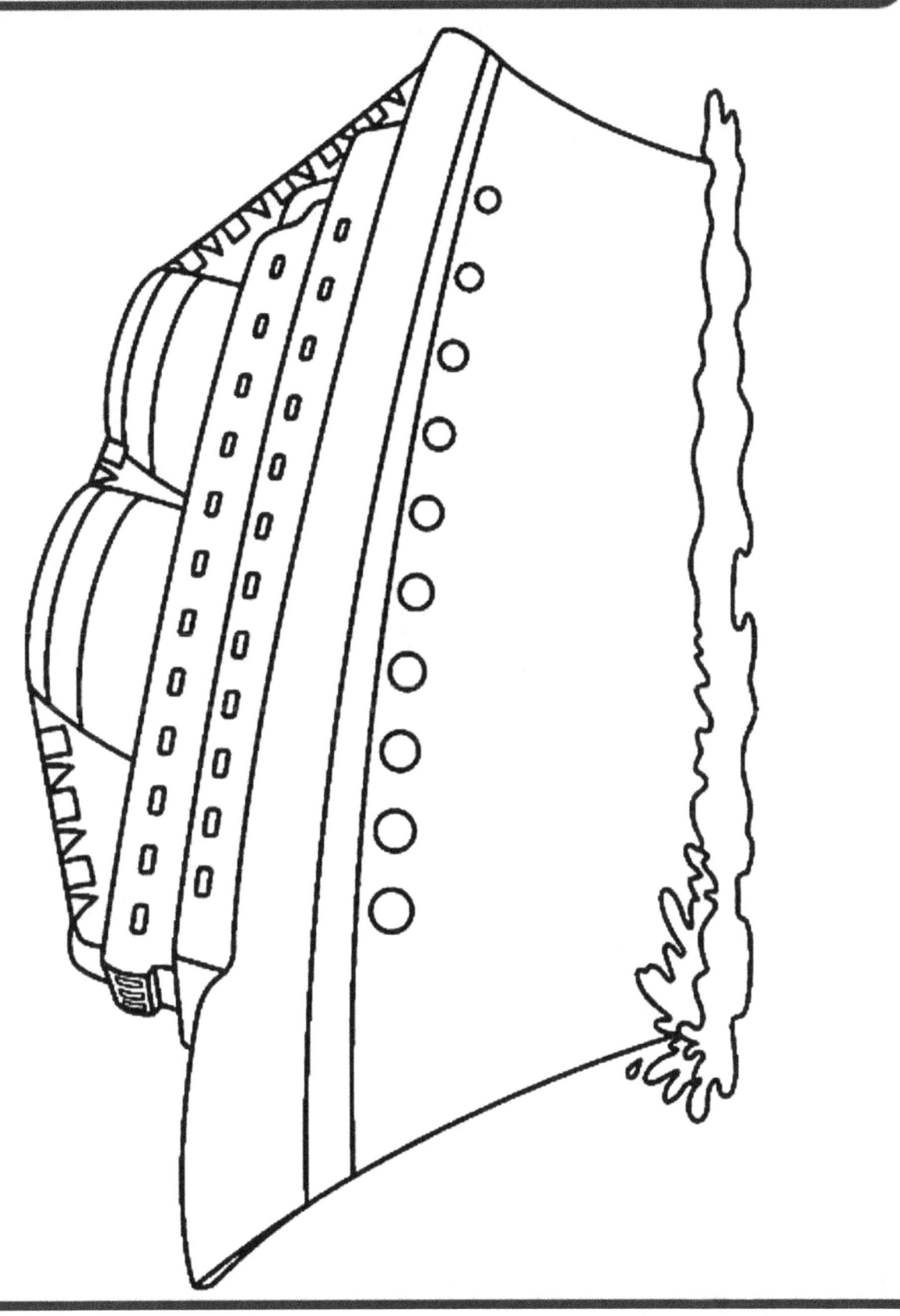

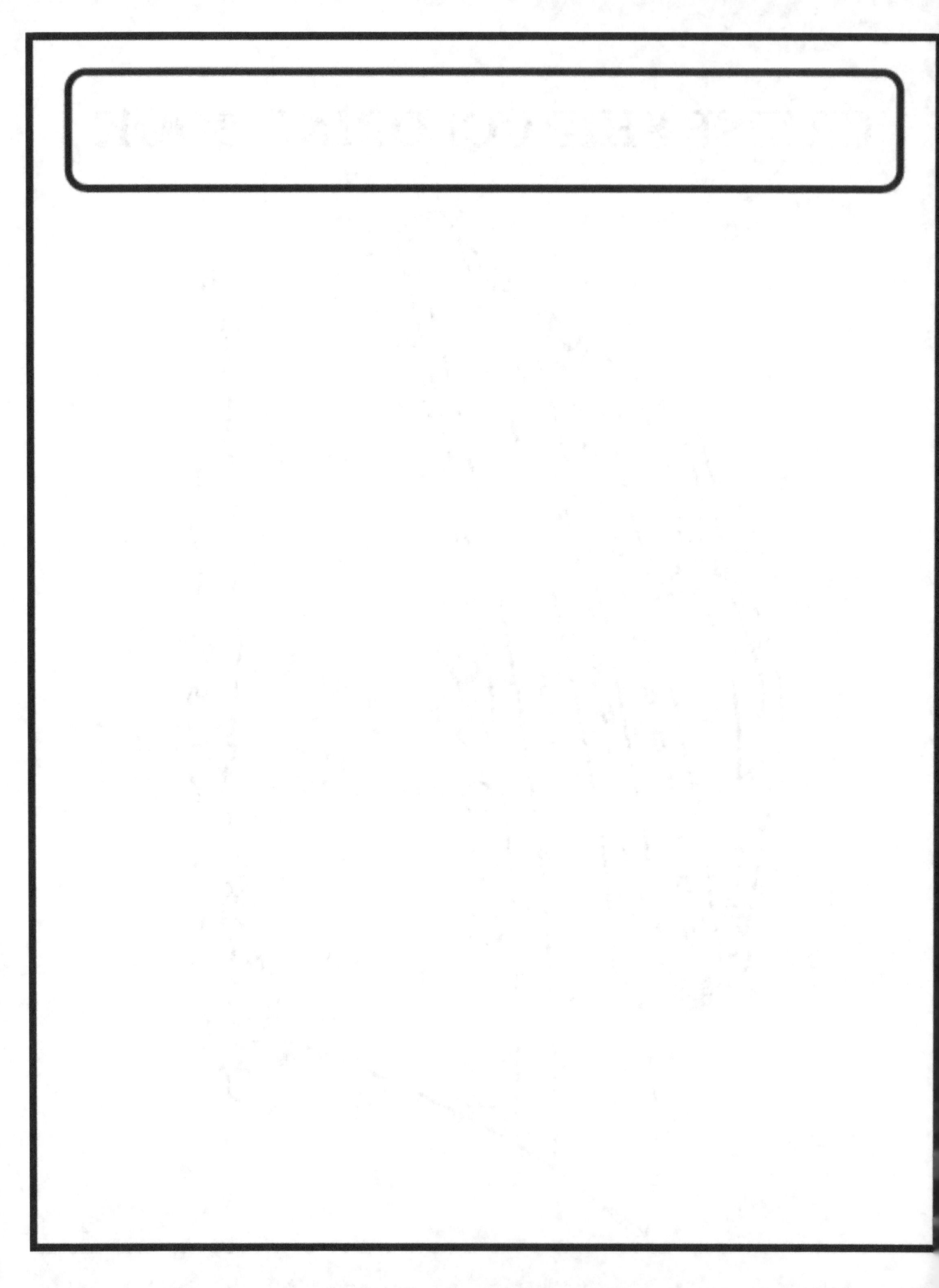

# CRUISE SHIP COLORING BOOK

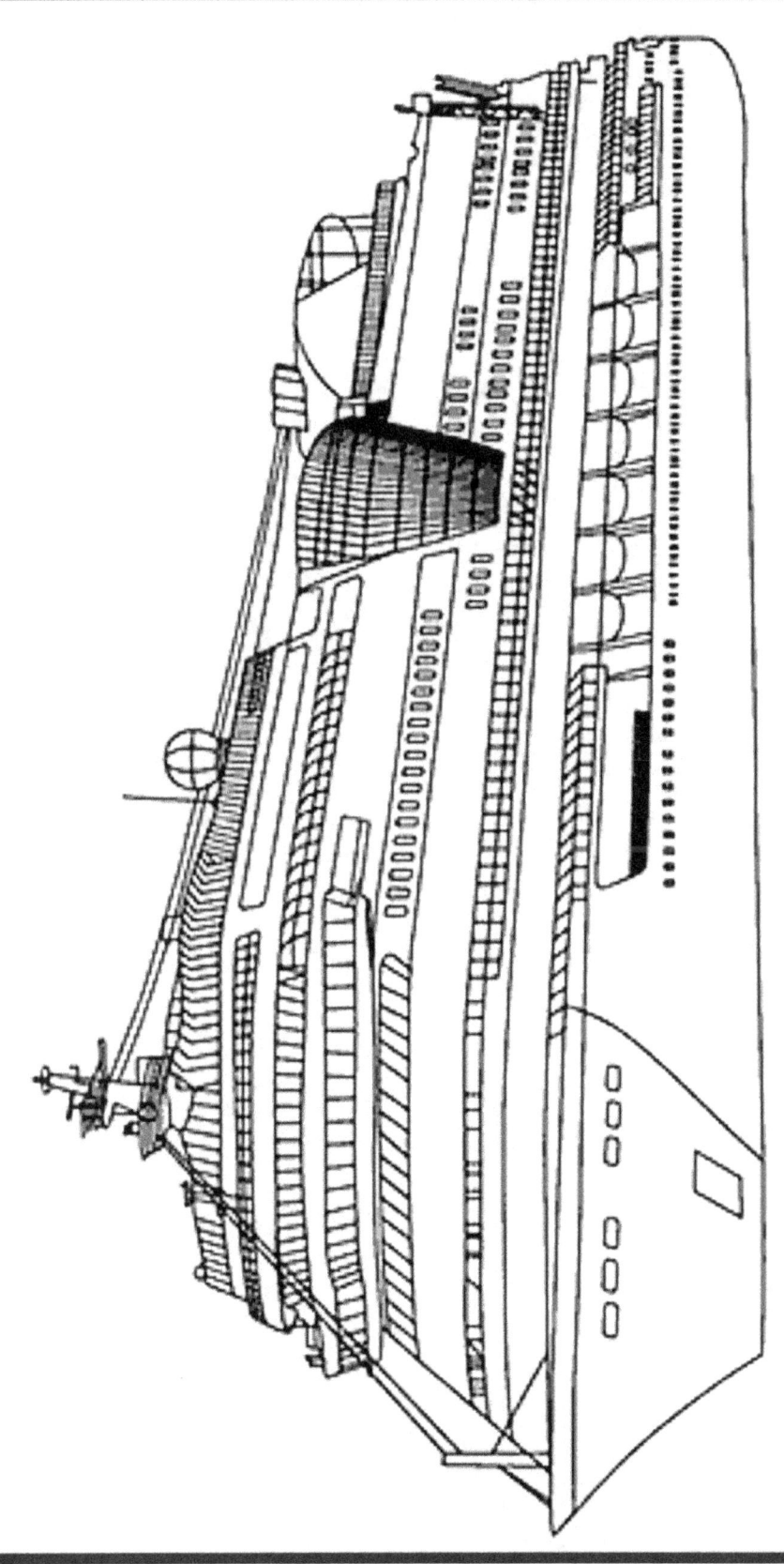

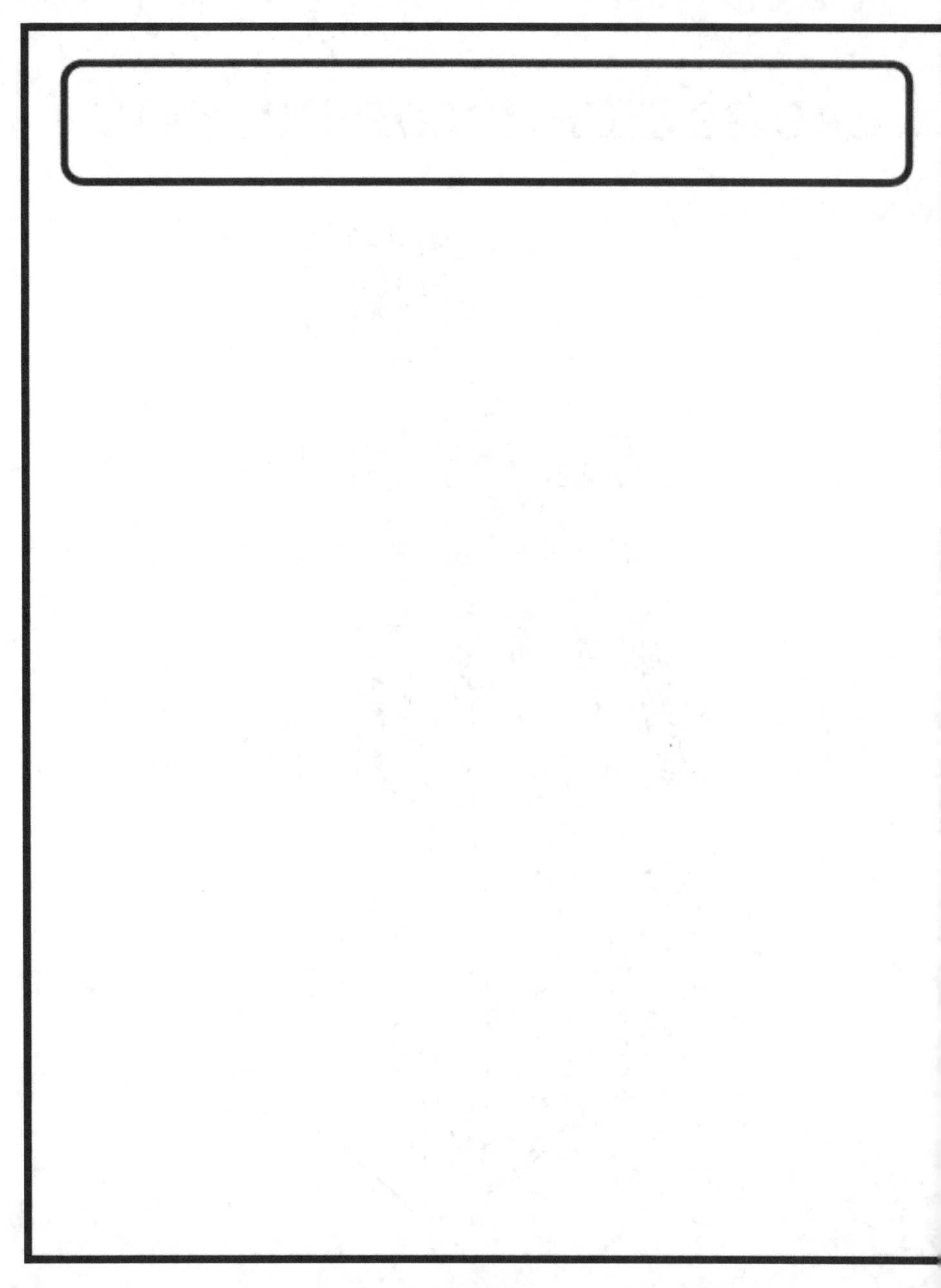

# CRUISE SHIP COLORING BOOK

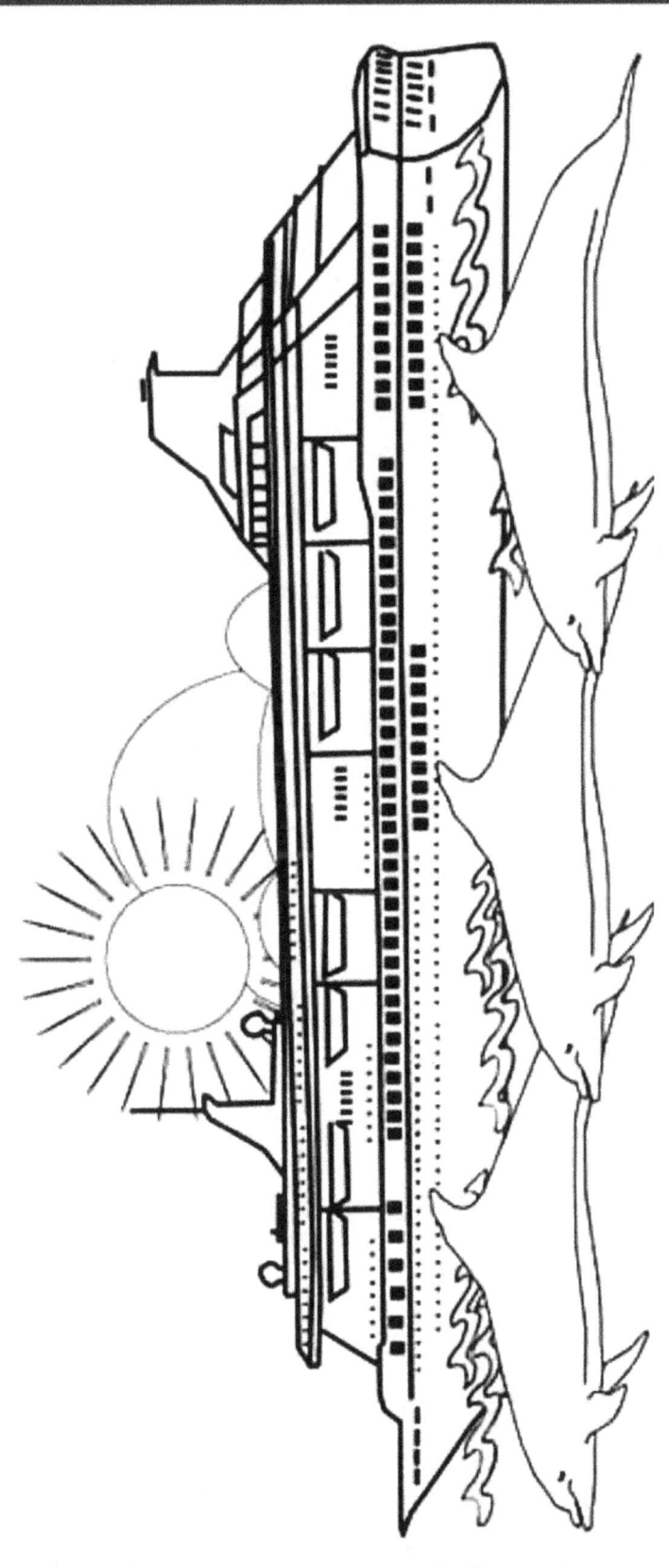

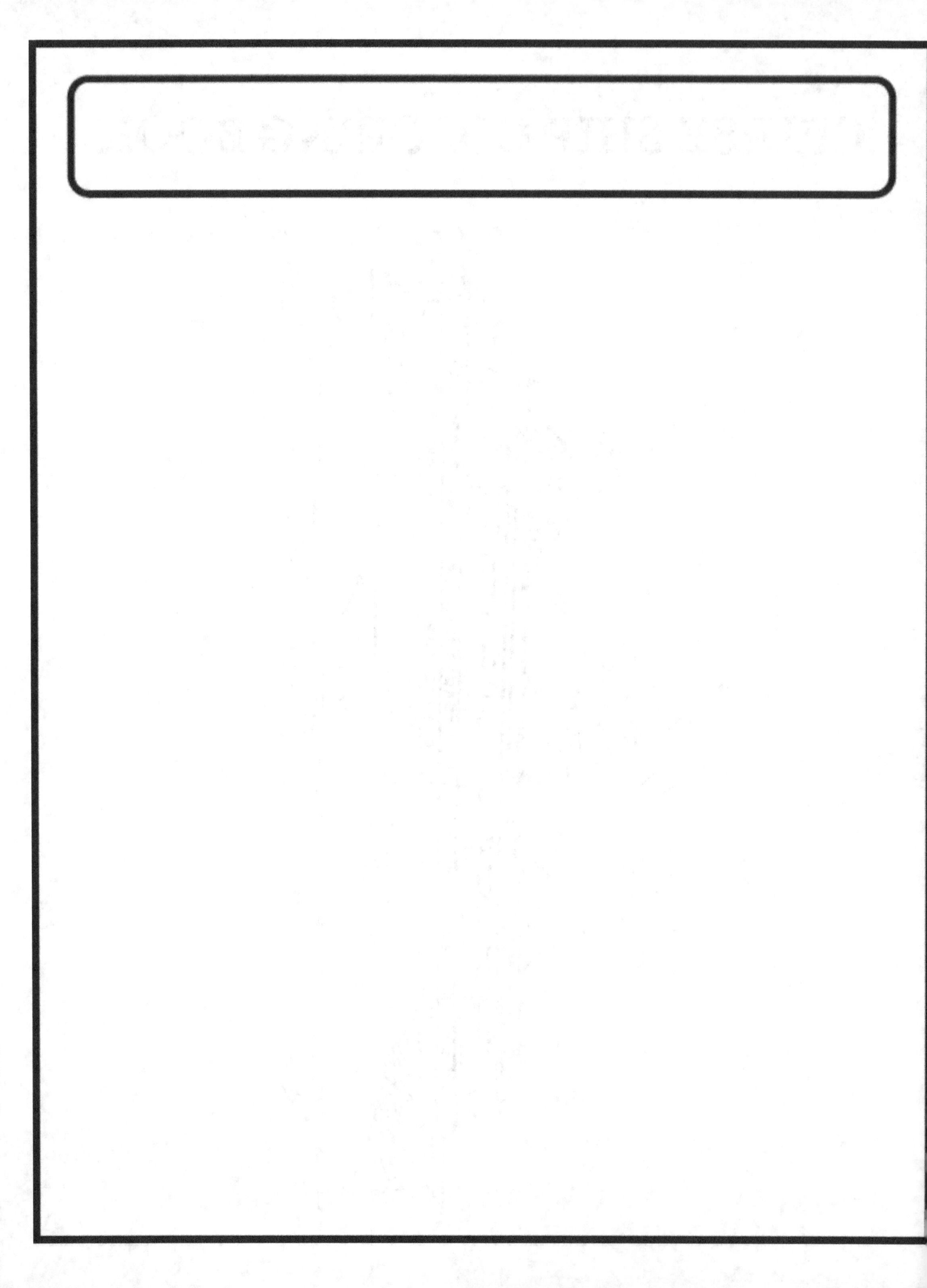

# CRUISE SHIP COLORING BOOK

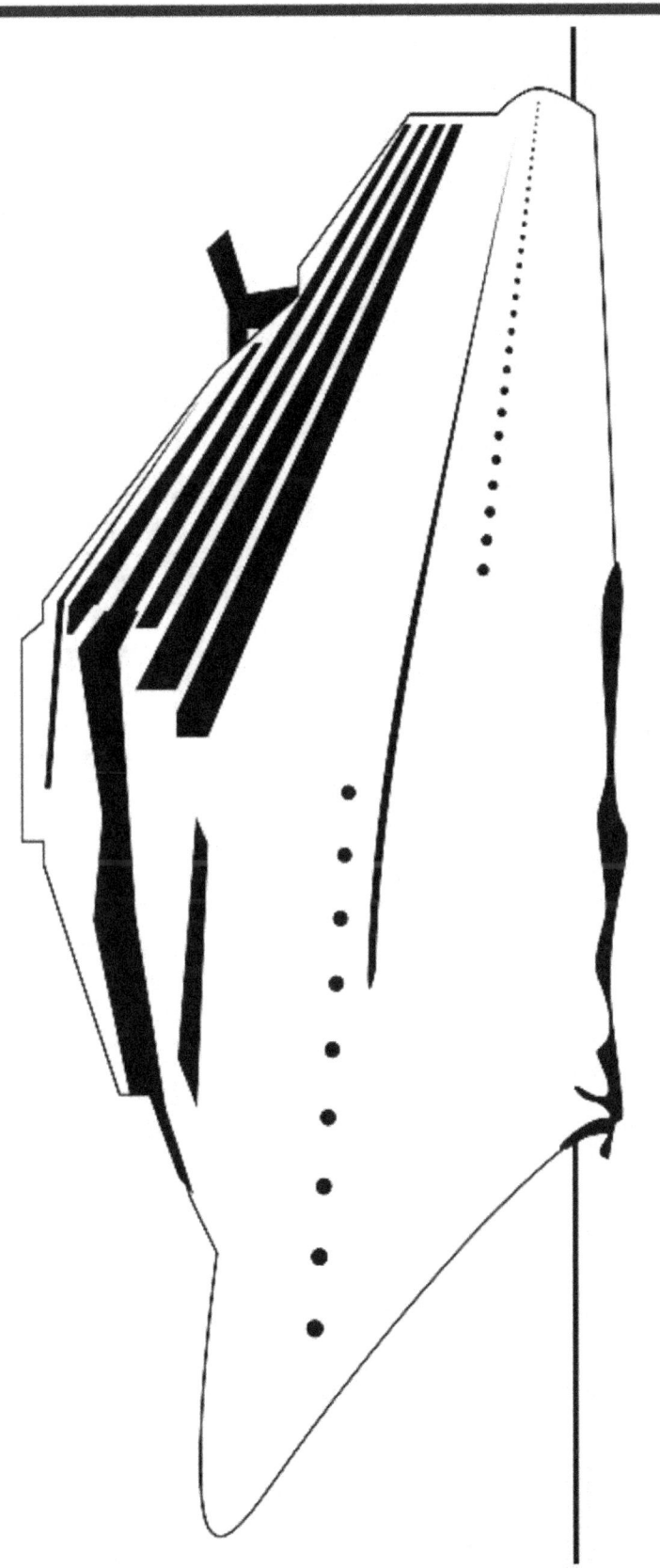

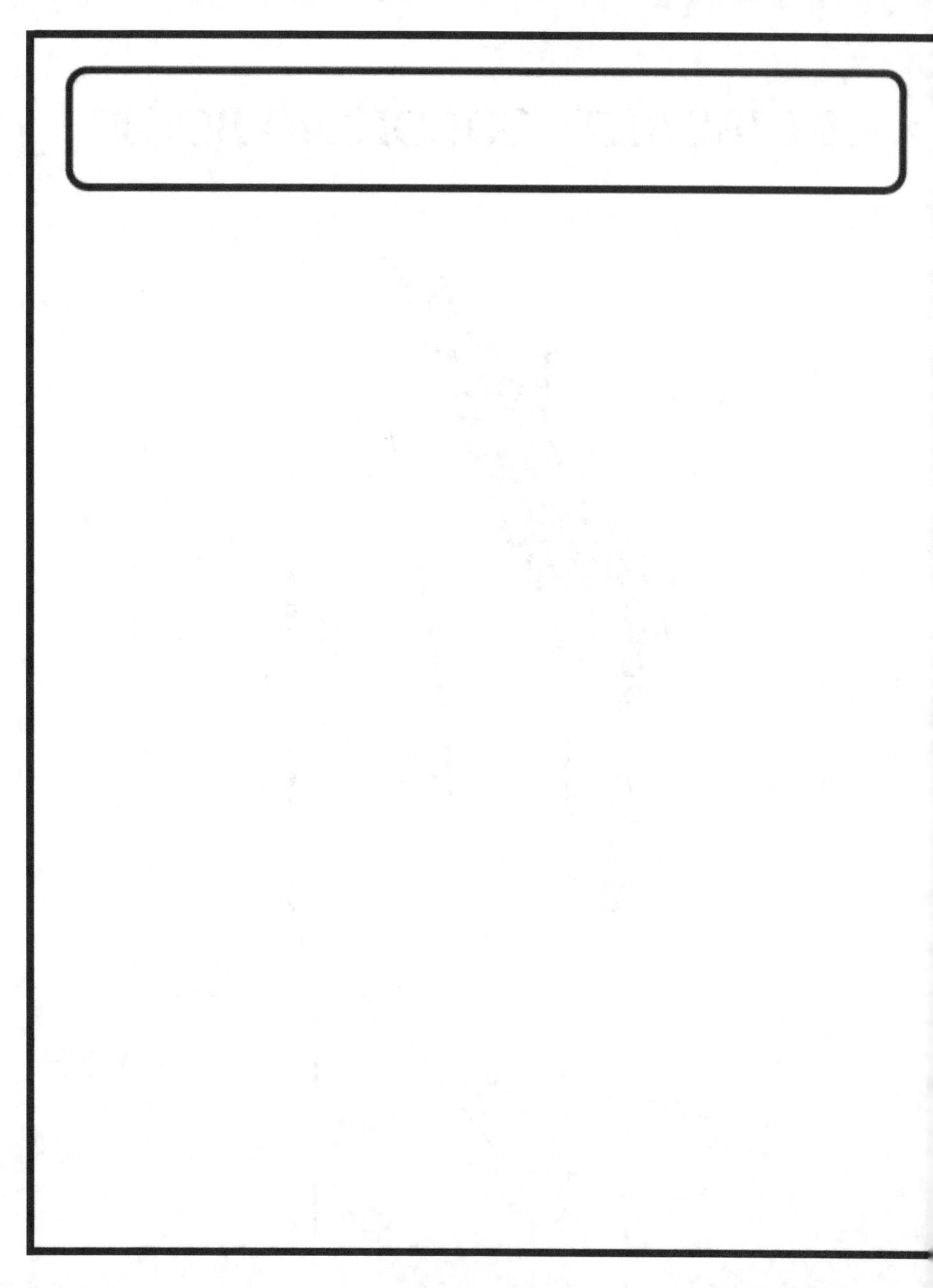

# CRUISE SHIP COLORING BOOK

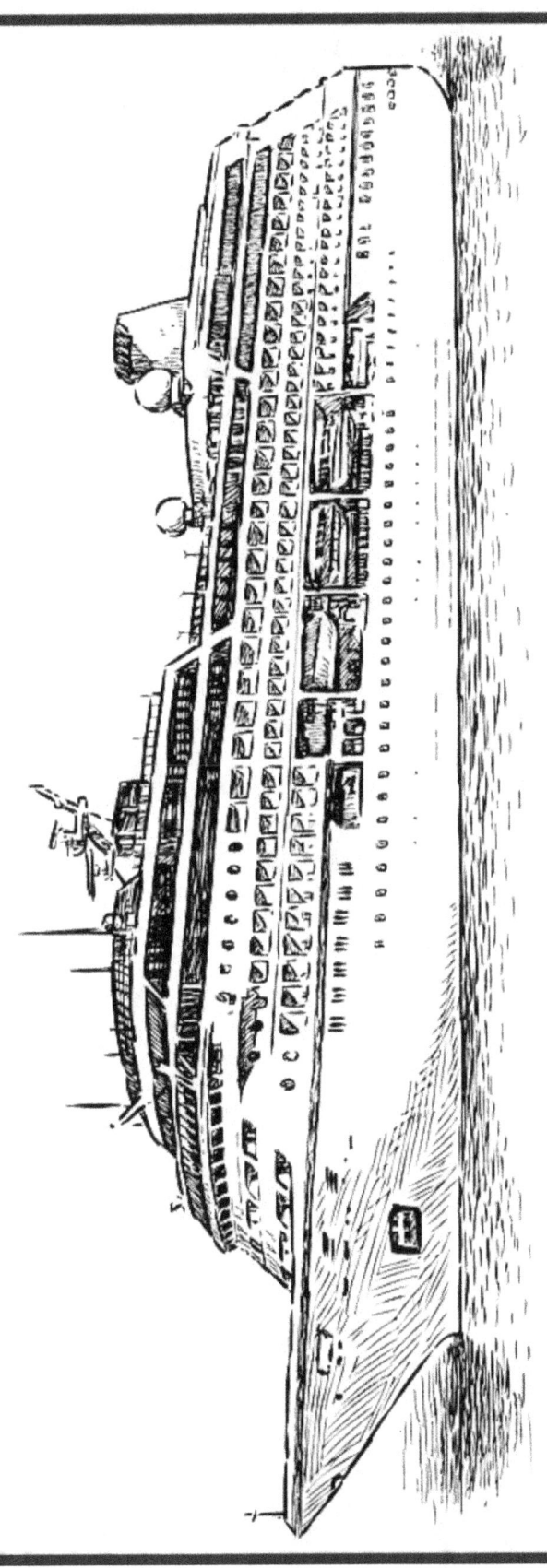

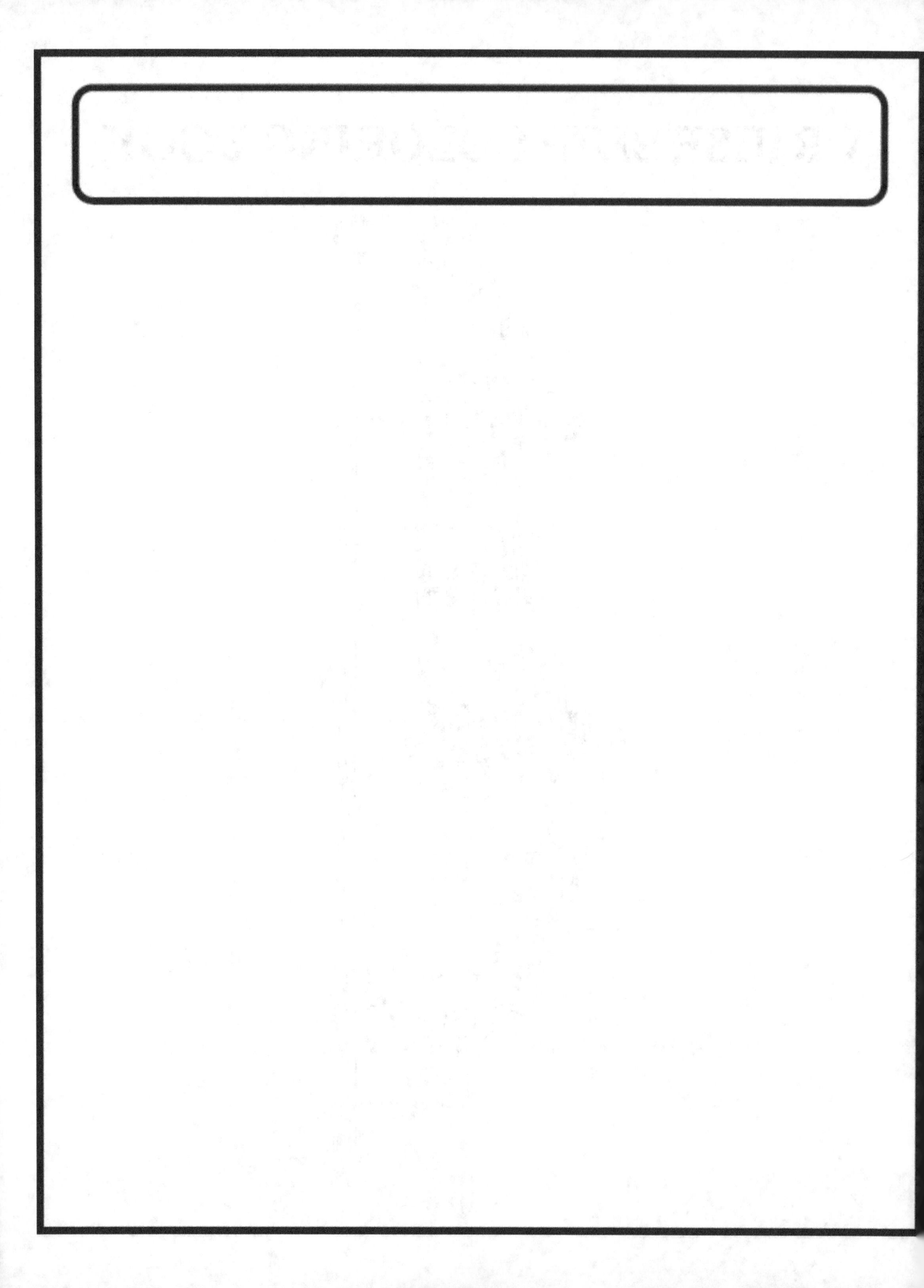

# CRUISE SHIP COLORING BOOK

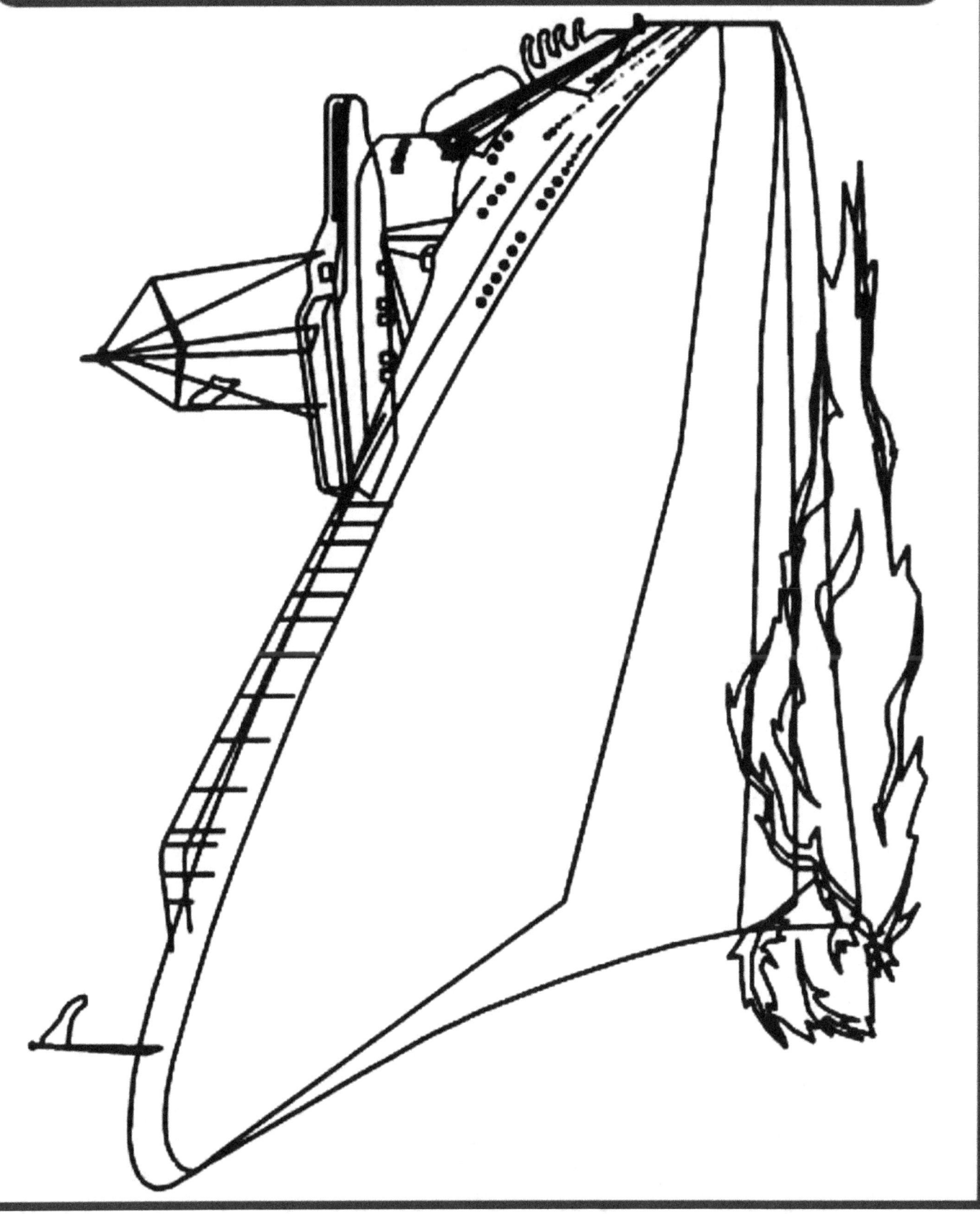

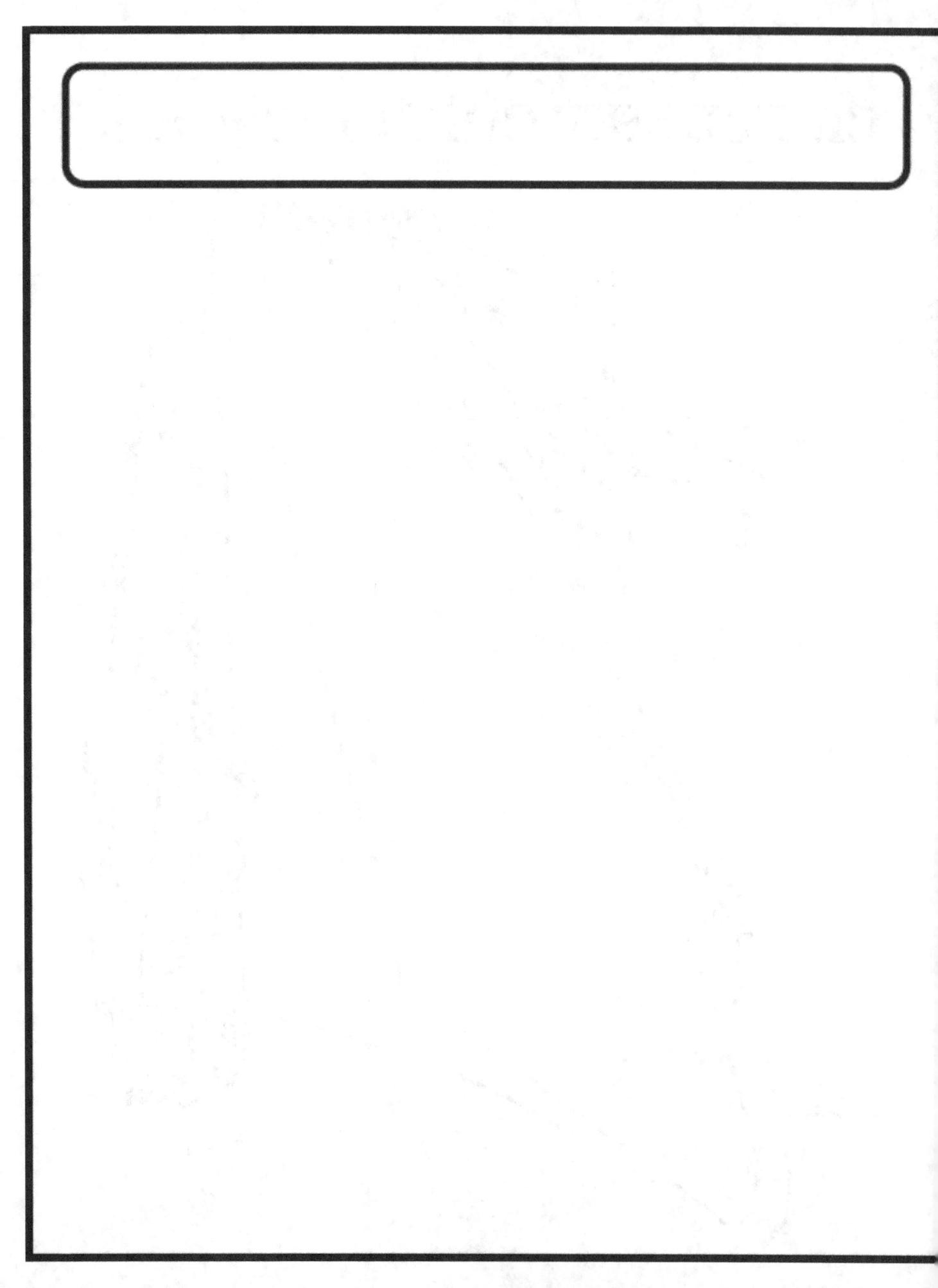

# CRUISE SHIP COLORING BOOK

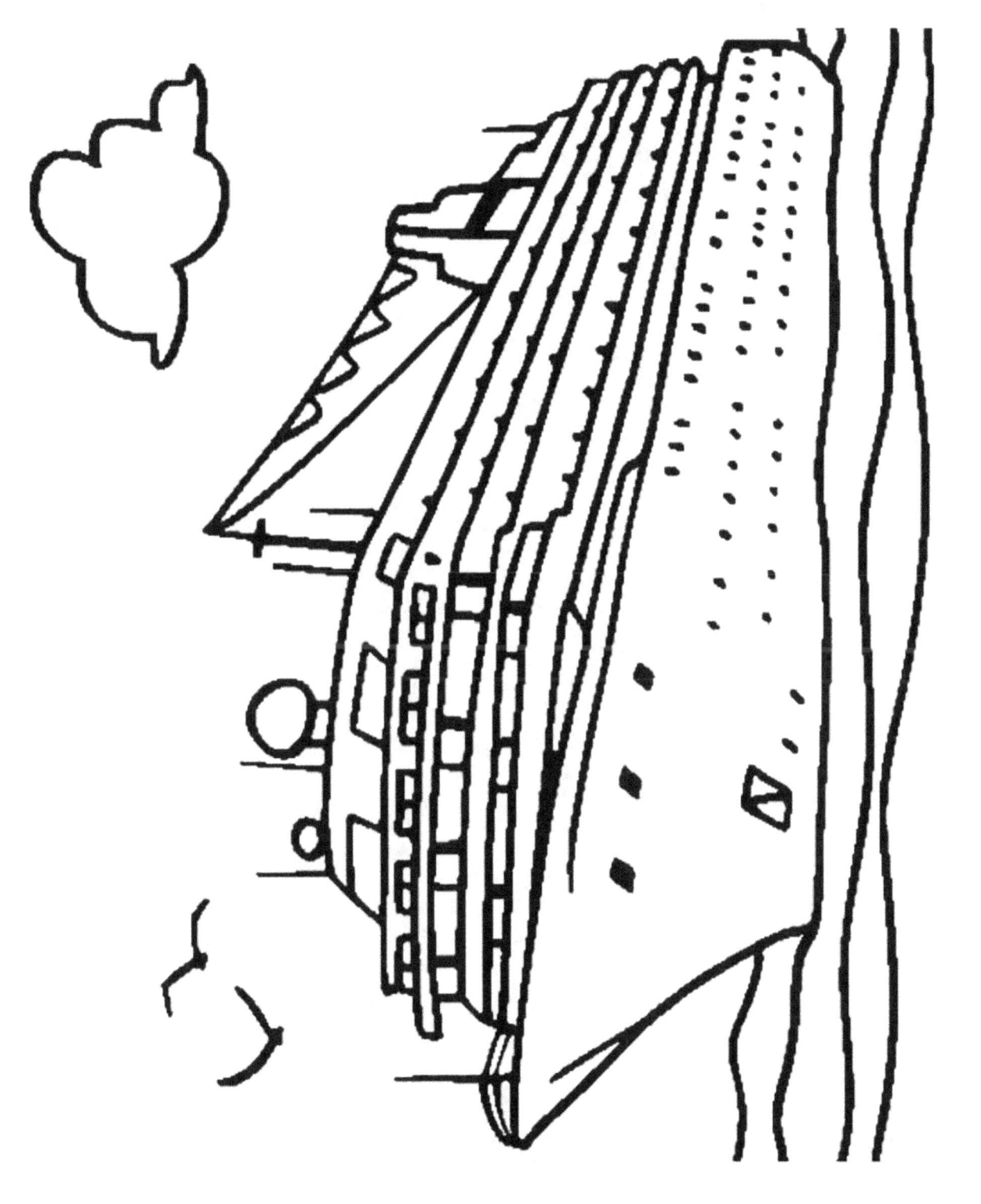

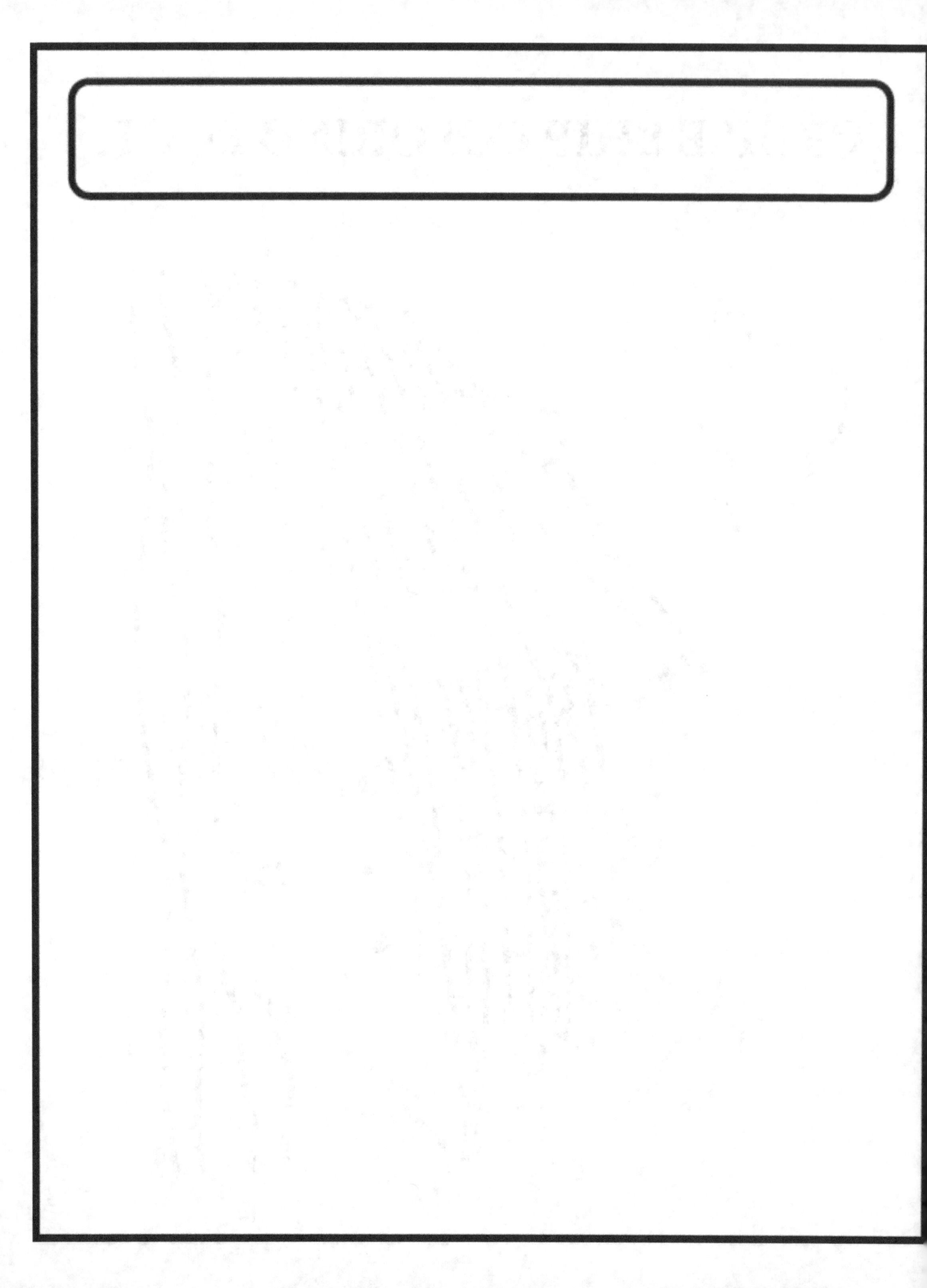

# CRUISE SHIP COLORING BOOK

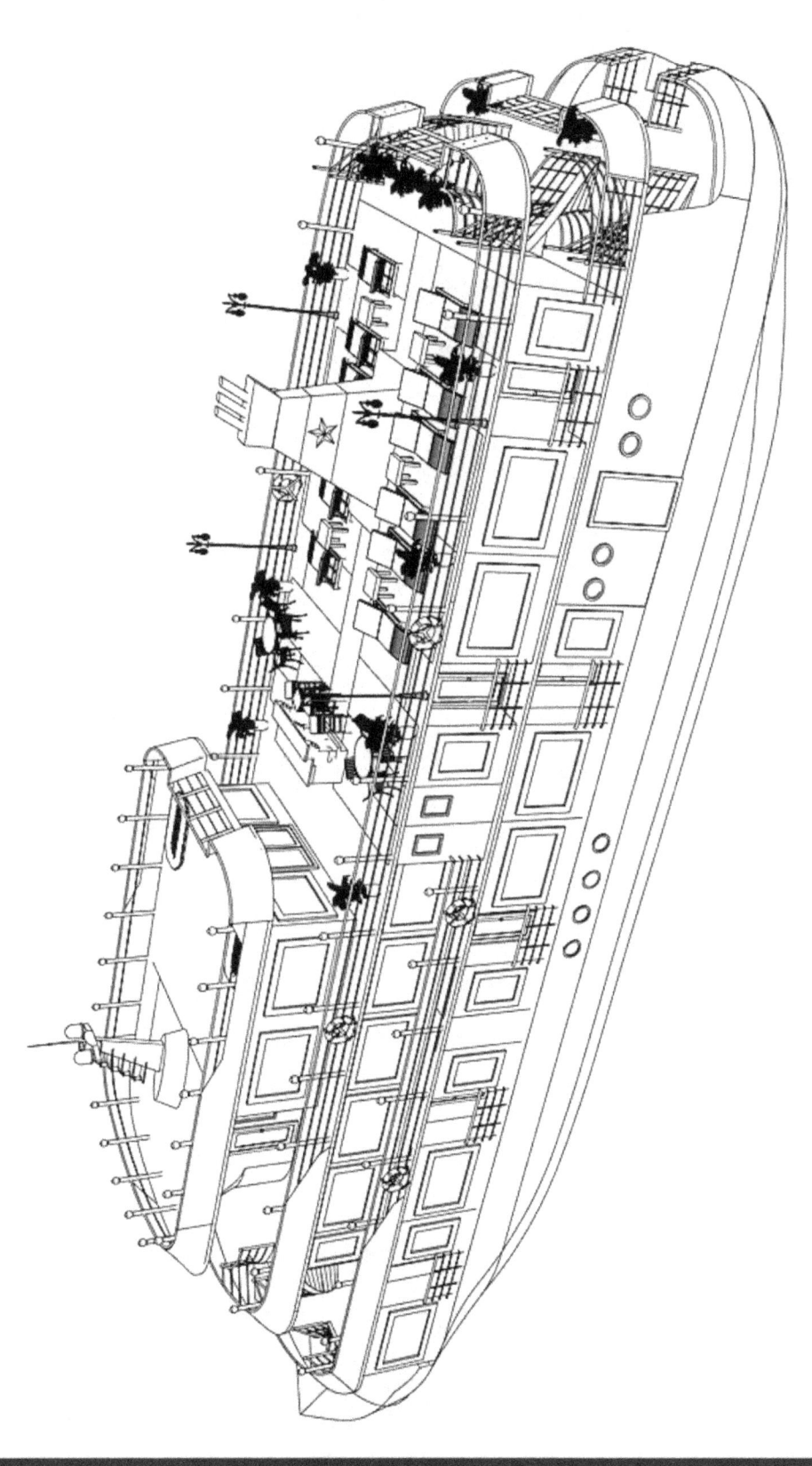

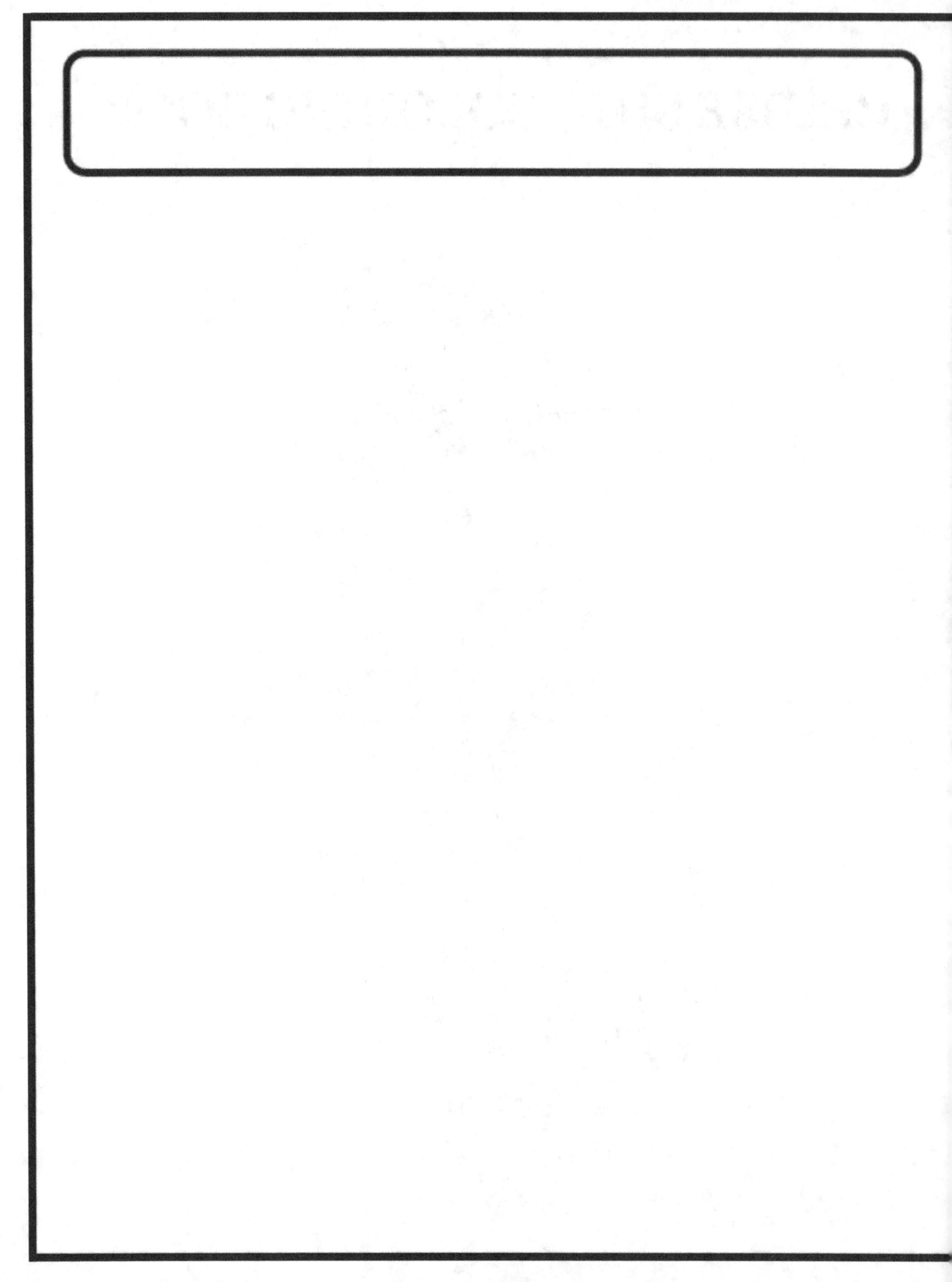

# CRUISE SHIP COLORING BOOK

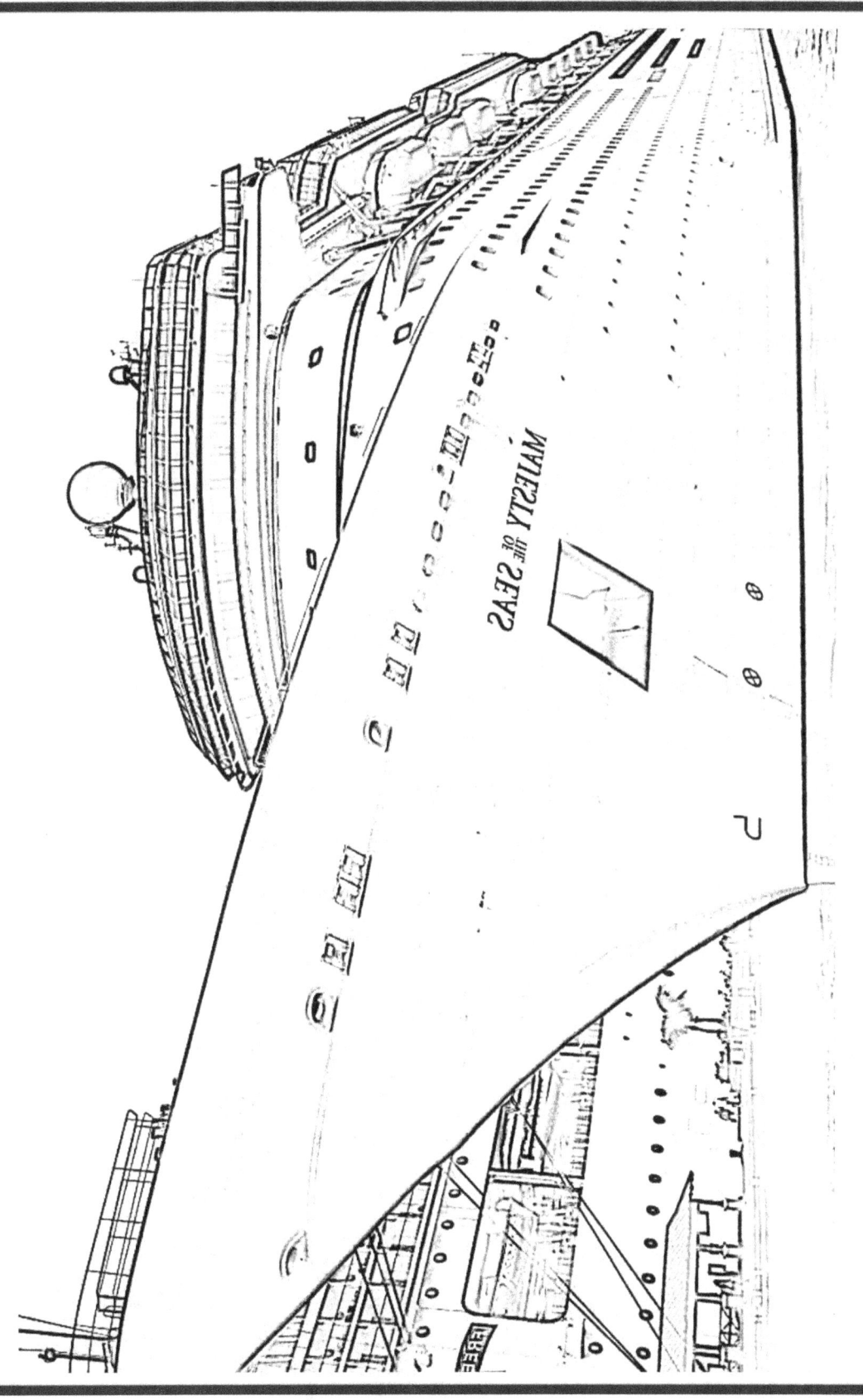

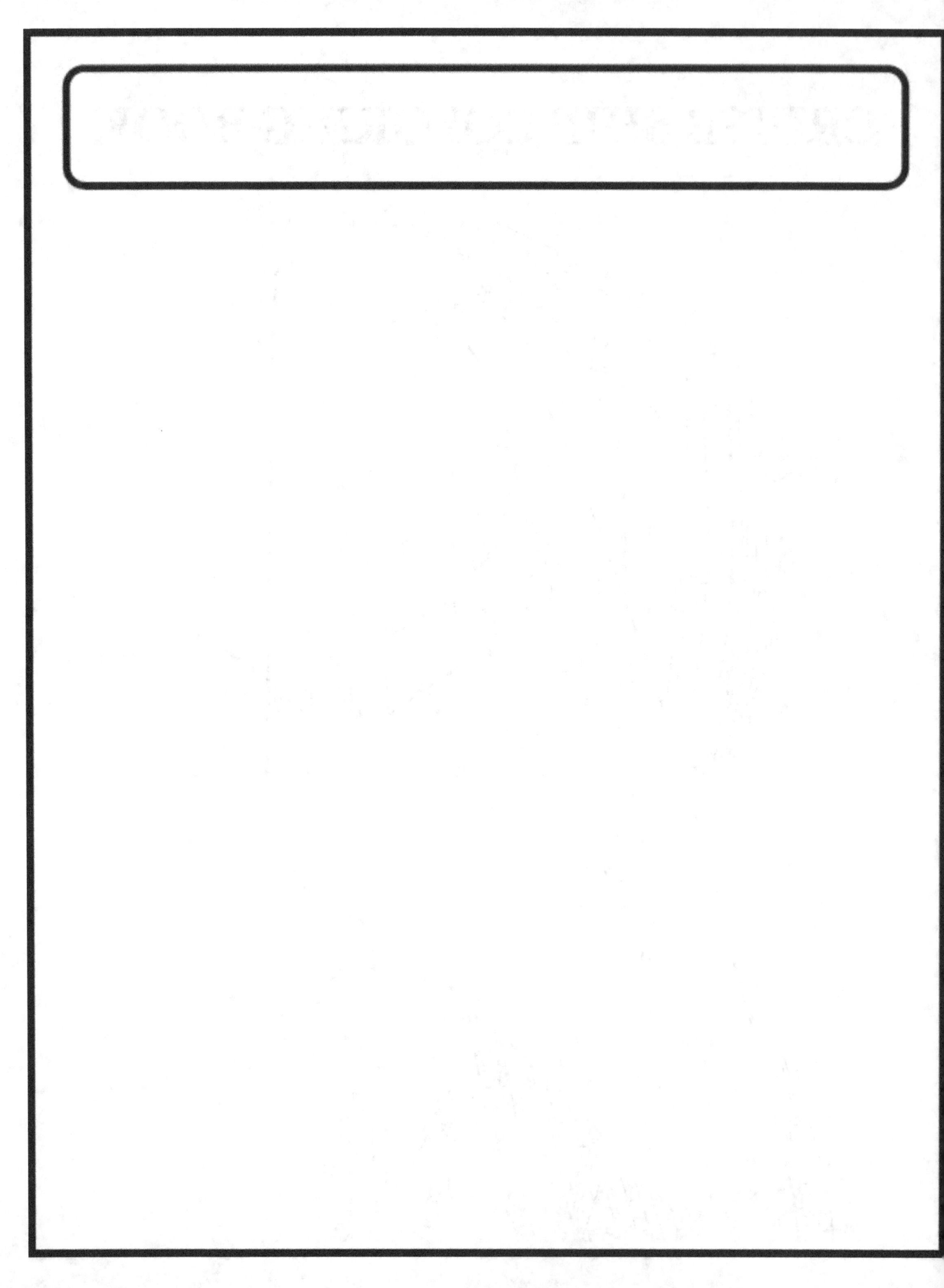

# CRUISE SHIP COLORING BOOK

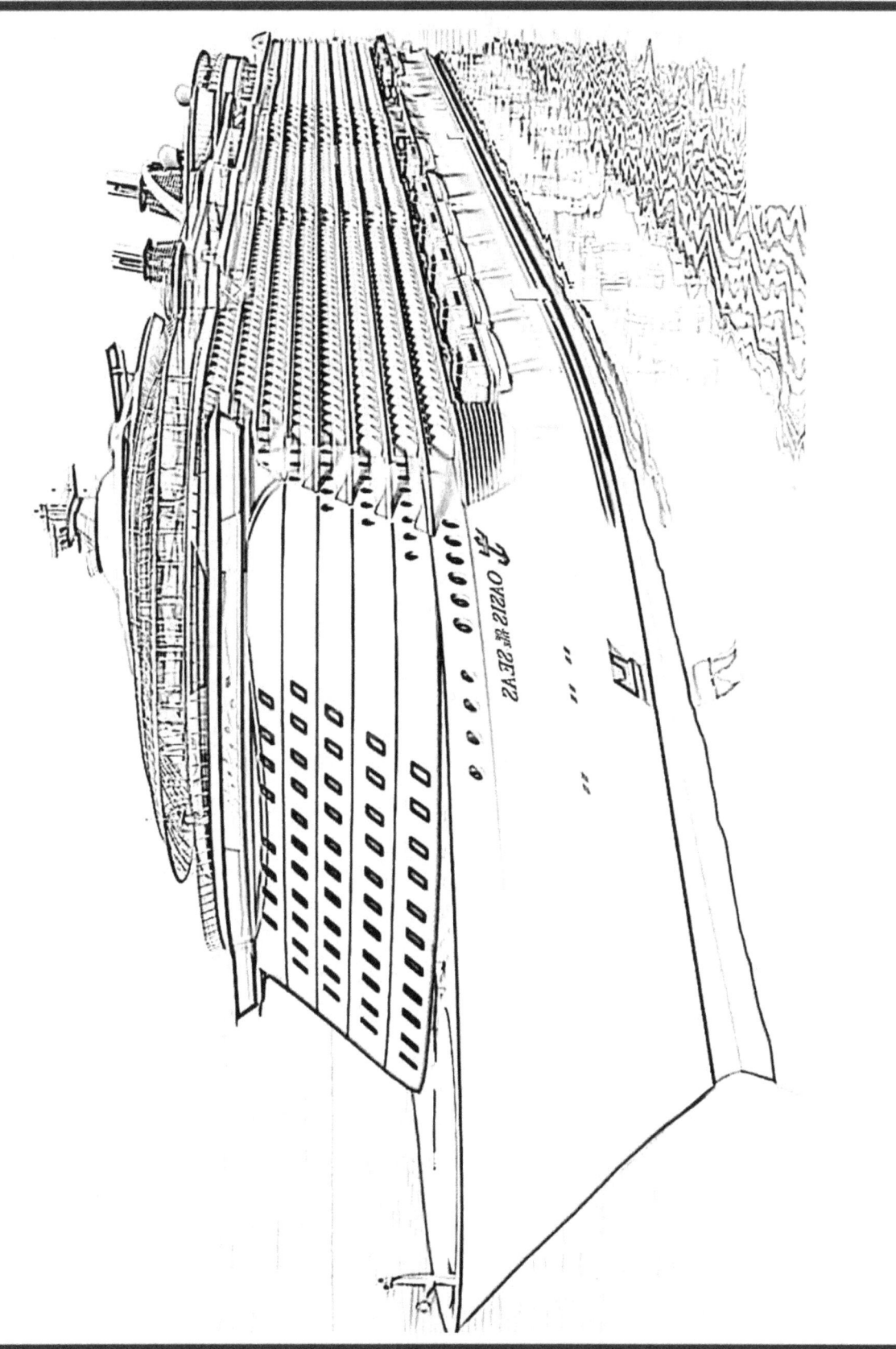

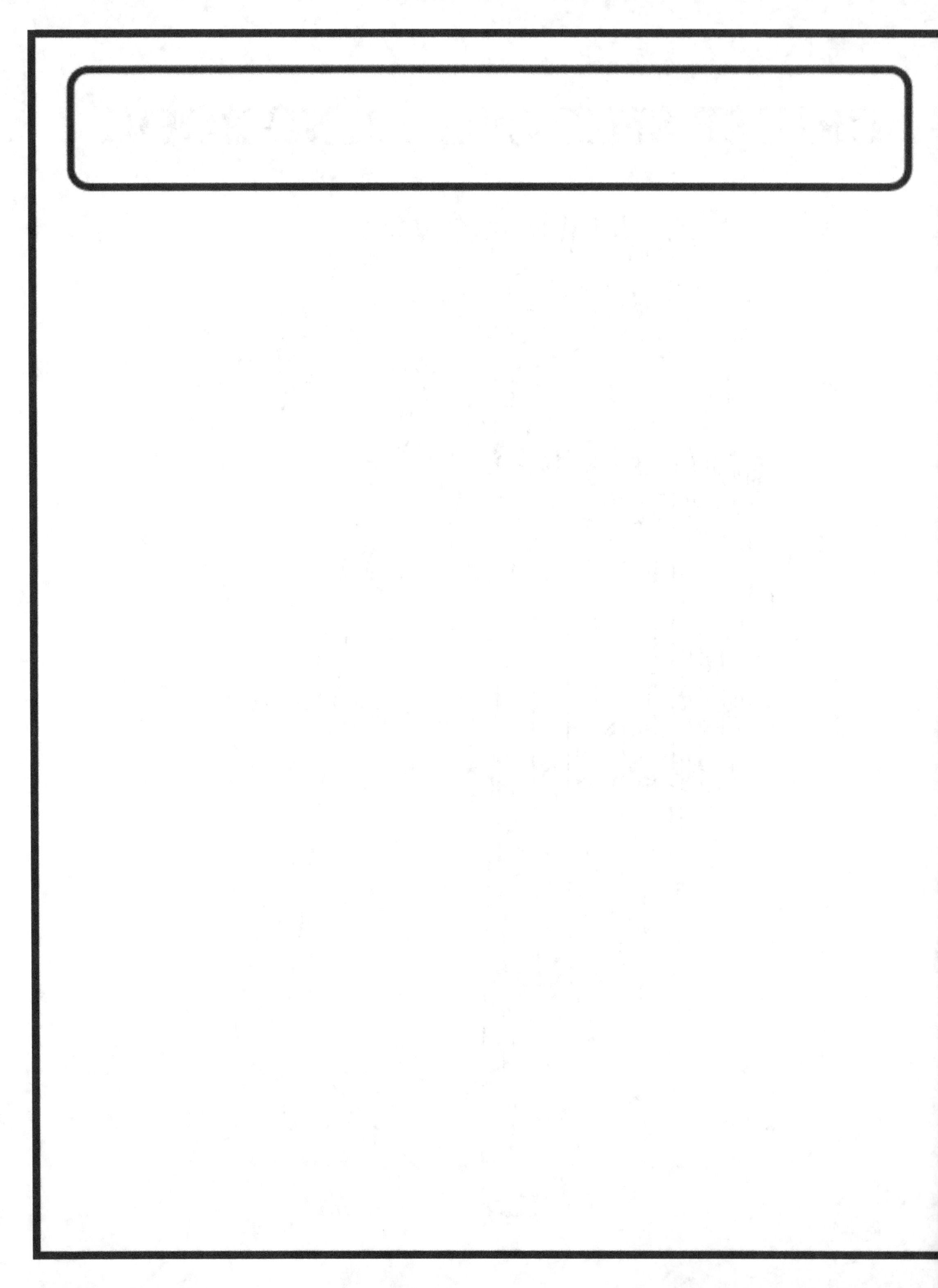

# CRUISE SHIP COLORING BOOK

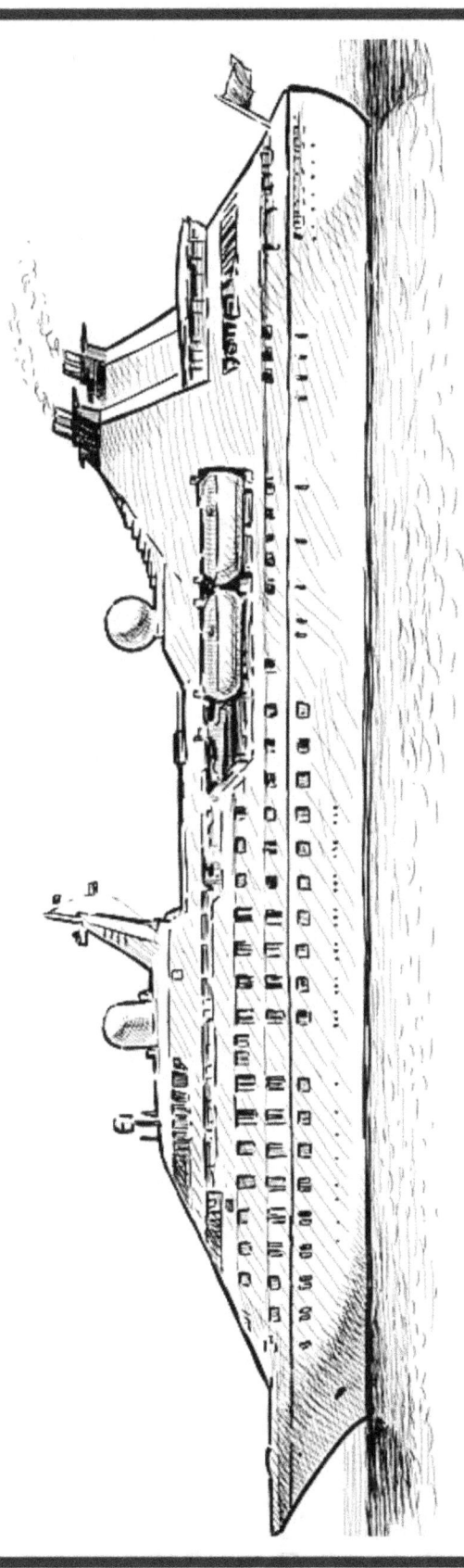

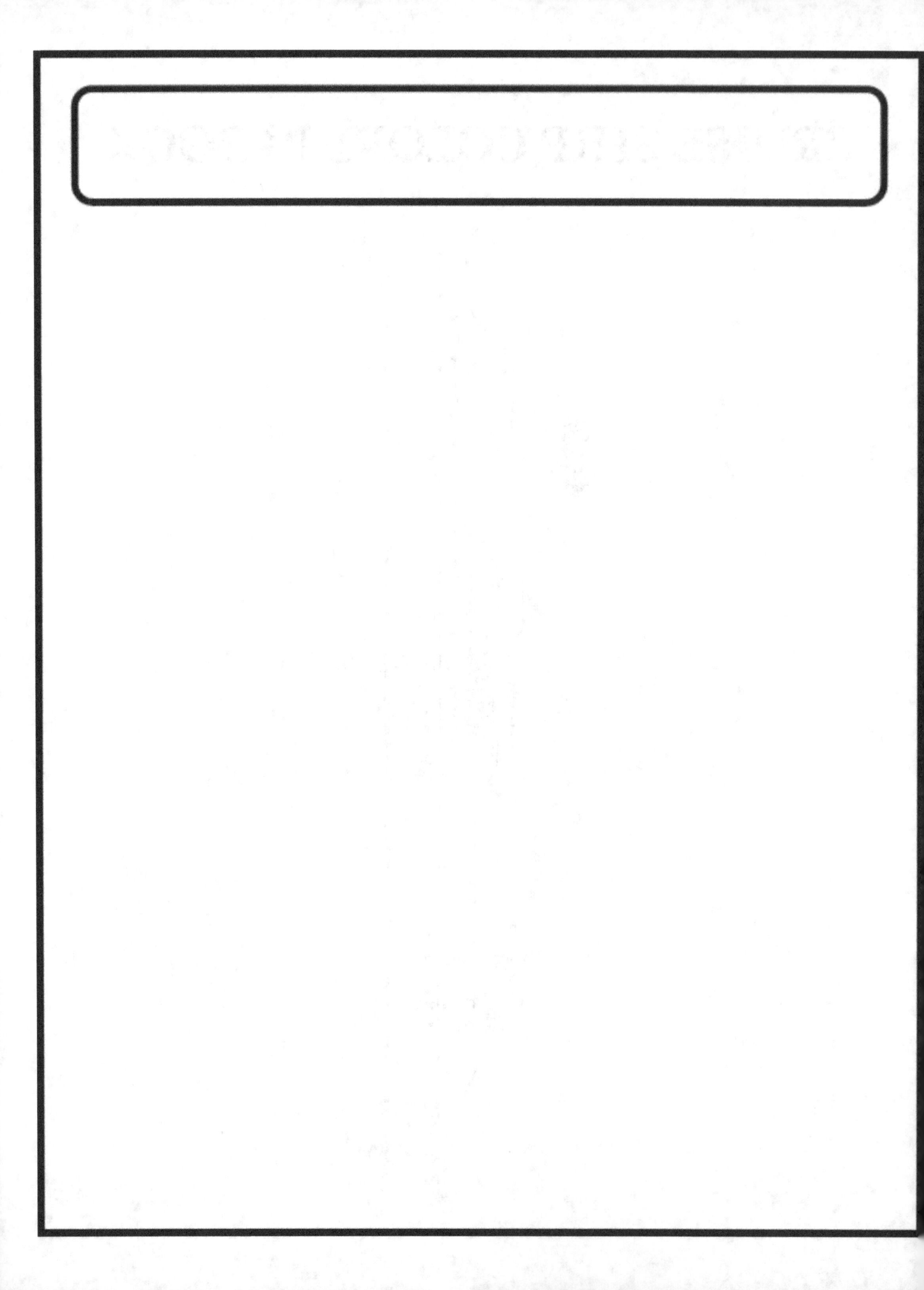

# CRUISE SHIP COLORING BOOK

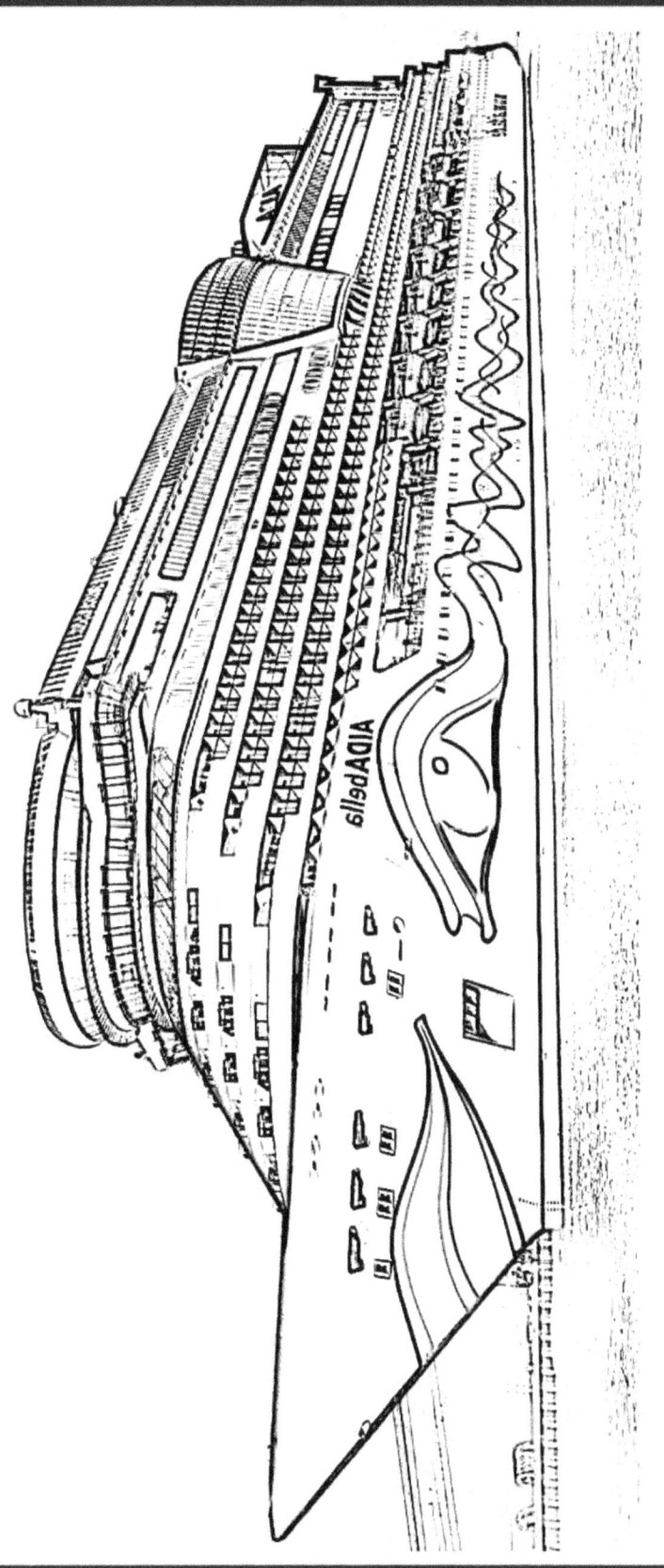

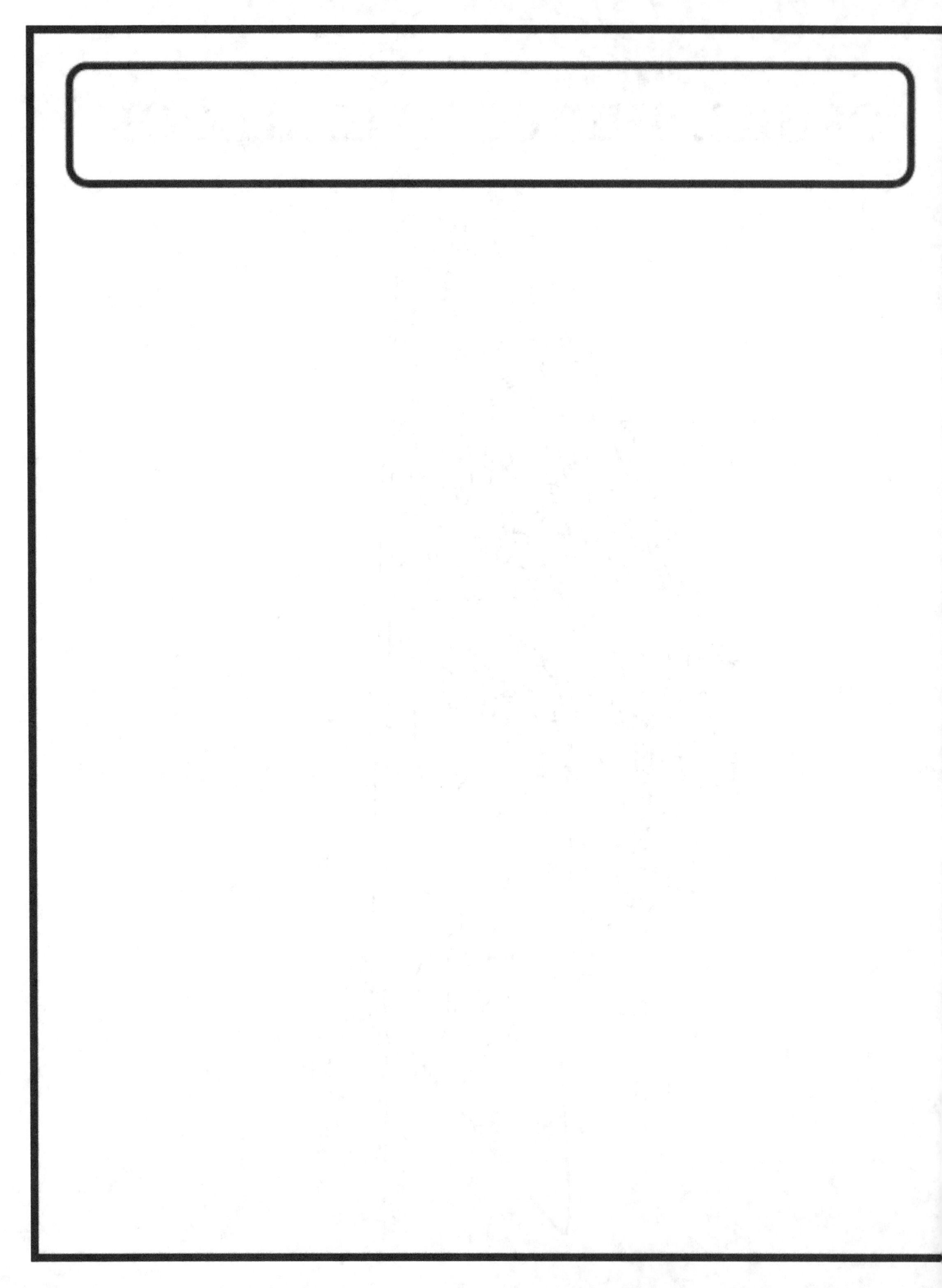

# CRUISE SHIP COLORING BOOK

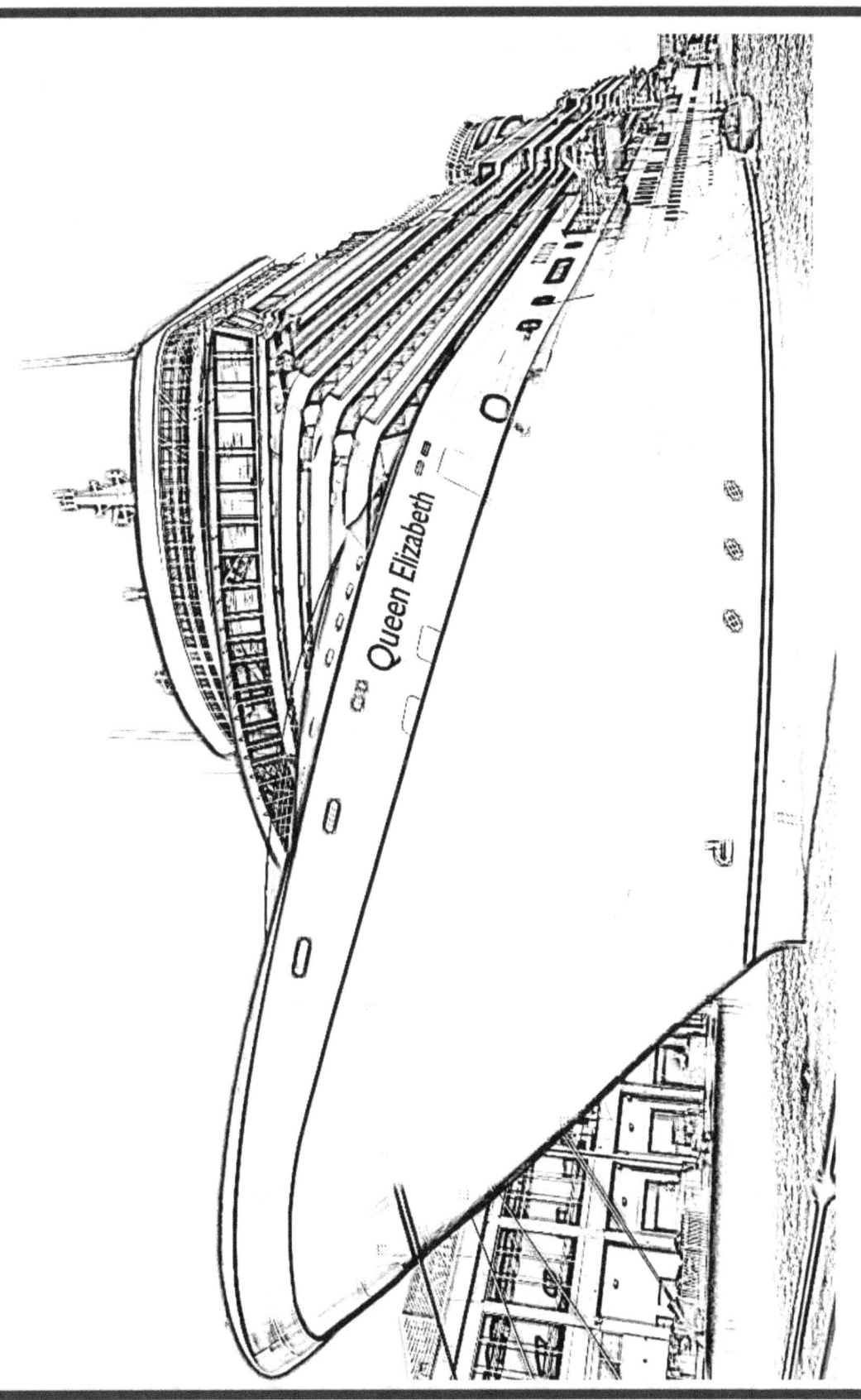

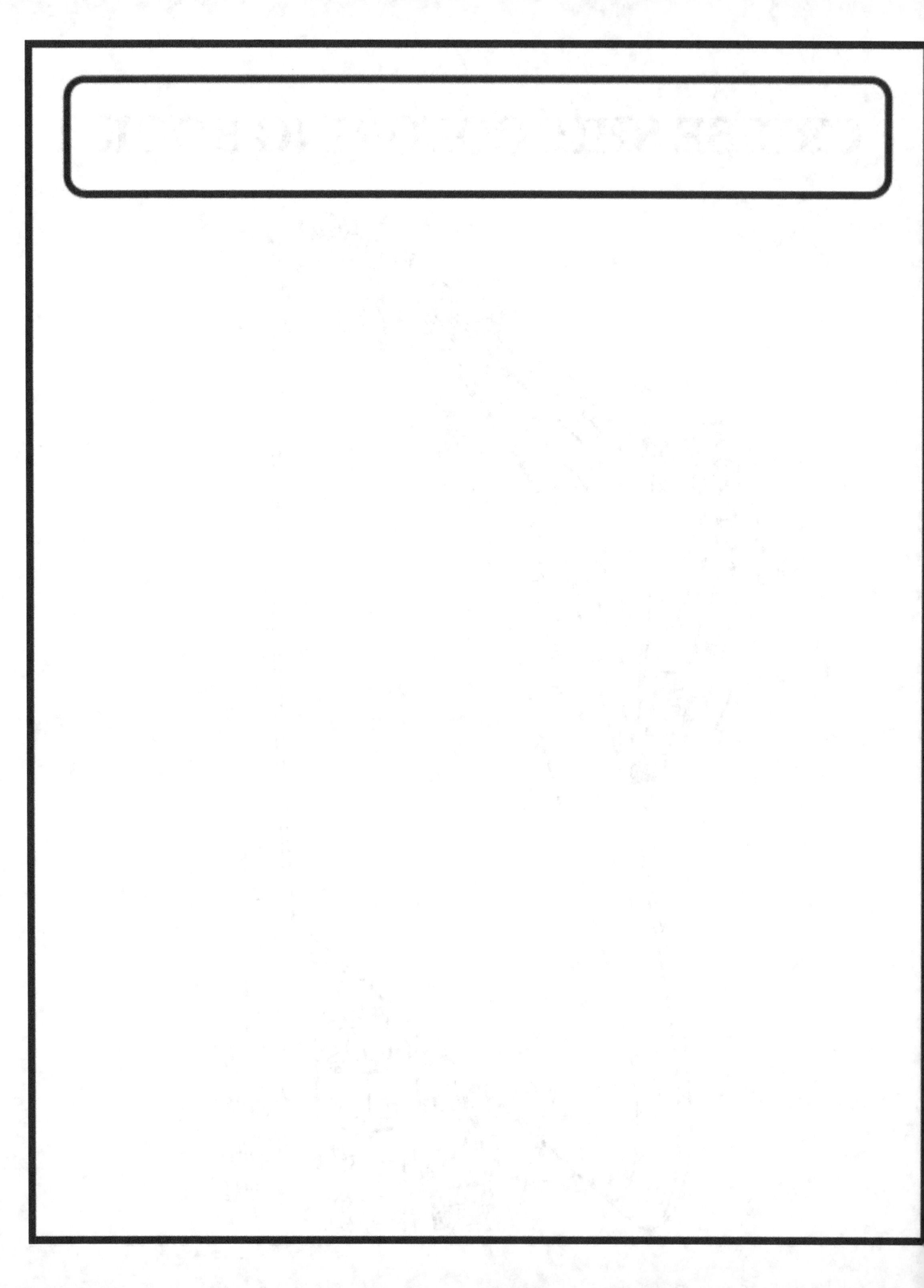

# Enjoying this Notebook?

Please leave *Black Rose Press House* a review
because we would love to know your thought,
feedback, and opinions to create
better products for you.
*Please share how you creatively use your
notebooks and journals.*

# THANKS
## FOR YOUR SUPPORT

*Scan This Qr Code And Visit Our
Author Page At-*
amazon.com

www.ingramcontent.com/pod-product-compliance
Lightning Source LLC
Chambersburg PA
CBHW08085220526
45467CB00008B/2517